The Setting in Life for *The Arbiter* of John Philoponos,

Sixth Century Alexandrian Scientist

by

John Emory McKenna

Wipf and Stock Publishers
150 West Broadway • Eugene OR 97401

1998

The Setting in Life for *The Arbiter* of John Philoponos,
Sixth Century Alexandrian Scientist
By John Emory McKenna
Copyright©1998 by John Emory McKenna

ISBN: 1-57910-090-2

Printed by *Wipf and Stock Publishers* 1998
150 West Broadway • Eugene OR 97401

TABLE OF CONTENTS

Abbreviations

Acknowledgements

Abstract

ABBREVIATIONS

AIVS	Atti del Real Institute Veneto de Scienze
ATR	Anglican Theological Review
BAB.L	Bulletin del' academie royale de Belgique
Bess	Bessarione
CD	K. Barth, Church Dogmatics
CH	Church History
DOP	Dumbarton Oaks Papers
DTC	Dictionnaire de Theologie Catholique
ISBE	International Standard Bible Encyclopedia
JAOS	Journal of the American Oriental Society
JEA	Journal of Egyptian Archaeology
JEH	Journal of Ecclesiastical History
JNES	Journal of Near Eastern Studies
JP	W. Böhm, Johannes Philoponos, Grammatikos von Alexandrien
MDIAA	Mitteilungen des deutschen Institut für ägyptische Altertumskunde
PG	Patrologia Graeco-Latina
PO	Patrologia Orientalis
PZ	Physikalische Zeitschrift
REG	Revue des études grecques
SP	Studia Patristica
ZNTW	Zeitschrift für die Neutestamentliche Wissenschaft

ACKNOWLEDGEMENTS

A work like mine is not possible without the good will and support of a
community whose faith is generously invested in its individual members.
Both freedom and responsibility must be nourished and respected for creativity actually to occur. The Faculty and Staff of Fuller Theological Seminary have been for me that kind of encouragement and strength. I am deeply
grateful to them.

President David Allan Hubbard was from the time I arrived at Fuller in
1976, always a special friend to my Christian growth, and Professor Geoffrey W. Bromiley worked harder on my behalf than any student could ever
expect or ask of a mentor. Without their guidance and devotion to Christ, I
could not have made the progress that I have. At my side in much of the very
difficult learning of languages, Professor Frederick W. Bush was willing to
agonize with me on many levels, even in my naiveté, so that he seems to me
now more friend than mentor. I can only say that the disappointments in my
performance shall not reflect in any way upon their profound and gracious
concerns for my labors. I wish to thank them from the bottom of my heart.

It is good for every community to be an open structured organization capable of a dynamic interface with other communities and individuals. If Fuller
were not such a Seminary, my life would never have taken the direction it
has and this work would never have even been attempted. Without the influence of the 1982 Payton Lecturship at Fuller, when the Very Reverend Professor Thomas F. Torrance of Edinburgh came and taught us, I would never
have begun any attempt to understand the thought of John Philoponos. His
steady encouragement has been of unspeakable value to me. My reader will
easily discern that I consider him to be one of the most creative theologians
in the Church today. In a day when Christian integrity seems as lost upon the
world as can be, it has been a privilege to attempt to understand the concerns
of the Torrance family in Scotland.

I also need especially to acknowledge the generous help given to me by
Professors Richard Sorabji and Sebastian Brock of King's College. From a
distance, they did their best to bring me up to the task in philosophy and Syriac scholarship. I am a better evangelist than philosopher or linguist, and for
them to help me in spite of my obvious weaknesses only speaks of the gener-
osity of spirit that truly exists in both of their fields.

I want most of all to thank my wife, Mickey, whose devotion towards me
and whose continual support has often picked me up when I was too weary to
go on. Together we have known how deeply people can hurt in this world and
we have known together the great and costly miracle it takes if people are to
have their wounds bound up and soothed and healed, that in the depths of their
being they may be restored to a life that is given to the praise of God. Thank
you, dear Mickey.

When I first wrote my dissertation, many friends helped us along in an
endeavor few could understand. They made difficult time better. Kathy
Patterson and Valarie Bush typed the original manuscript upon which I have
now worked a little in order to see the argument published, after ten years

5

of seeking a way to get it before the community of faith. Anybody who has ever written a dissertation knows how invaluable they were to me. Now that my work will be published, I must publicly thank John Wipf and John Stock for their courage to see John Philoponos become better known and their understanding of my efforts to argue the way that I have.

Finally, in the providence of God, the publishing of this work would not have possible without the surprising support of the Worldwide Church of God, with whom I have labored now for two years as her leaders have sought to respond fully to the grace of God they have freshly grasped in our time. To President and General Pastor Joseph Tkach, his Executive Advisor Michael Feazell, and to Dr. Russell K. Duke, now the Director of the Worldwide Church of God's Ambassador Center at Azusa Pacific University, I offer my salute, both for their courage and their willingness to support me in the ministry of the Gospel of Jesus Christ.

But then there is God to thank, who in spite of all our rebellion against Him passionately seeks still to be known for who He truly is in the midst of our world with us.

Rev. Dr. John E. McKenna
Worldwide Church of God
Pasadena, California
November, 1997

ABSTRACT

The background for the writing of *The Arbiter* (Διατητής) by John Philoponos, a sixth-century Alexandrian scientist, is explored. The Anathema of the Grammarian at the Academy of Alexandria is first studied. Monophysites in the East and Chalcedonians in the West both found his argument for the Person of Jesus Christ unacceptable to the Church. An analysis of this condemnation is given. Then the historical development of the theological concerns that led up to the Fifth Ecumenical Council, summoned to Constantinople in 553 AD by the Emperor Justinian, is studied. It is claimed that Philoponos was appointed by royal command to act as the umpire in the debates between Monophysites and Chalcedonians with a view towards their reconciliation. His response to the royal appointment cannot be understood without apprehending the scientific culture in which Philoponos labored. This is, therefore, next investigated, and the revolutionary concepts developed by John are shown to depend profoundly upon his Christian beliefs. It is then argued that the expression of the Person of Christ found in The Arbiter cannot be grasped without understanding the scientific concepts employed by the Grammarian against the Ptolemaic Cosmology and Aristotelian Physics popular in his day. The study suggests that the anathema of the Alexandrian Scientist by the Church is a mistake, comparable to the treatment of Galileo, which if it were to be righted, and a fresh translation and interpretation of The Arbiter were to be made, would prove a valuable contribution to modern efforts to resolve Christological problems and the struggle of contemporary thought to produce a Doctrine of God which takes into account the real nature of the world.

7

"... as wretched John the Grammarian, raving with wisdom gone astray, and exalting himself against the God-clad fathers...."

-- Peter of Callinicum (586 AD)
tr. Ebied, R. Y., Van Roey, A., and Wickham, L. R.

"Philoponus' philosophy found no echo in his time, and twelve hundred years has to pass until the impact of Galileo's ideas brought about a complete change in scientific thought."

--Shmuel Sambursky, (1975 AD)
in *Physical Thought from the Prescratics to the Quantum Physicists*, p. 45

CHAPTER ONE

THE ANATHEMA

At the Imperial command of Constantine Pogonatus, the Sixth Ecumenical Council of the Catholic Church of Jesus Christ was convened on the 7th of November, 680 AD in Constantinople, the capitol of the Byzantine Empire. Some three hundred bishops were summoned together in order to define once again, in continuity with the inspired Councils of the Church at Nicea (325 AD), Constantinople I (381 AD), Ephesus (431 AD), Chalcedon (451 AD), and Constantinople II (553 AD), the Rule of Faith outside of which existed every kind of heresy and abomination. Famed for their condemnation of a Roman Pope, the Holy Fathers were gathered especially to consider that extension of the Christological debates which continued to rage between Monophysites and Orthodox in the East and the faithful in the Western Church, debates which had reached their most exquisite form in a struggle against Monotheliticism. The Council pronounced anathemas upon Arians, Appollinarians, Eutychians, Timotheans, Acephali, Theodosians, and the Gaianitae, along with all heretical madness which attempted blasphemously to think together the two natures, divine and human, in the union which was the person of Jesus Christ. The Holy Fathers insisted in no uncertain terms that there was and only could be two wills, and not one will, according to the natures of Christ. All those who would explain the unity of the Christ in such a manner as to suggest there was only one will were anathematized,[1] the culmination of a struggle by which the Church attempted to guard the Apostolic Faith handed down by the Holy Fathers to those who would come to know the salvation of God. It is, perhaps, appropriate to remember from the start that

9

the certainty with which the Council proclaimed its belief in the way they had been able to express their thought of the Person of Christ never was and is not now universally shared.[2]

Included among the lists of heretics was Severus, Patriarch of Antioch during the years 512-518 AD. Severus is considered to be the greatest Neo-Chalcedonian theologian in the Eastern Church of the Sixth Century.[3] He spent his early life intending to become a lawyer, but was influenced by Peter of Iberia into an anti-Chalcedonian communion and became a monk instead.[4] He sought to interpret for his time the Christology of Cyril of Alexandria in the understanding that the Tome of Leo tended to conceive the two natures of Chalcedon's confession in a Nestorian manner, a sophistry which had been unmasked by Cyril and condemned in 451 AD. Severus had employed the term "nature," when he sought to think together the divine nature of the One Triune God with the human nature of Christ, in such a way that the term 'nature' ought to refer to the "essence" or "being" sometimes, and sometimes to signify specifically the hypostasis of a given individual reality.[5] The "incarnate nature" of Cyrillian Christology was, according to the hypostatic union, one nature which simultaneously must refer to the humanity of Jesus and the divinity of the Eternal Son, the Word which had become flesh. Thus, the person of Christ was considered one reality, even though He was of two natures. Severus liked to use an analogy of light in order to help him explain how we may learn to think in this way about Christ. The Son was the Eternal Ray of the Glory of the Father as sunlight is to sun, that is one in essence or being and two in hypostatic realities, which may not be confused. He uses this analogy to establish the Father as the hypostatic mind, the Word as the hypostatic Son, and the Spirit as the hypostatic Spirit of the One Creator. It was the hypostasis of the Word which incarnated and not the Father or the Spirit.

Thus, we must be able to conceive the divine nature of the Son as the hypostasis of the Word whose nature had become flesh or assumed humanity. Jesus of Nazareth is the hidden God, the darkness of the light, so to speak. The resurrected Christ is the light of light as the revelation of the Father, God seen in the flesh as He is in Himself, in a new relation to the created world announcing a new creation. Severus considers the hypostatic union to be the very ground of his own assumption into the real relations established for man in Christ with the Eternal God. For the Patriarch of Antioch, Leo's Tome did not appreciate the profundity of the significance of the hypostatic union. Up against the one profound reality of the Person of Jesus Christ, two natures, each functioning according to that which was appropriate to its nature, seemed merely a rationalization of a deep and saving wisdom.[6] For his contention with Chalcedon and the Tome, Severus was exiled from his See in 519 by Justin I and spent the last years of his life in Alexandria. He died there during the reign of Justinian in 538.

In the 7th Century, John of Damascus, generally considered to embody the culmination of Chalcedonian Orthodoxy in the Ancient Church, understood *The Arbiter* by John Philoponos as a work written in the tradition represented by Severus, and the Grammarian from Alexandria is included with the great theologian of the East among the Monophysite heretics.[7] The Damascene, by quoting from *The Arbiter*, has preserved for us a fragment of chapter four and chapter seven from the work. He considers that Philoponos presents "vain things," denying the mystery of salvation and being opposed to the 630 inspired Fathers of Chalcedon. He thinks the Grammarian "set many snares" and "laid stumbling blocks" which would "destroy the mystery of Incarnation." He claims both Severus and Philoponos are "lost in pernicious heresy" and belong to a "Godless and abominable here-

11

sy."[8] The fragments of *The Arbiter* quoted by the Damascene are those in which Philoponos attempted to define and explicate the crucial terms and significant problems which had arisen in the Church with the controversies over the natures and hypostasis of the person of Christ.[9] In the fourth chapter, attempting to characterize the relation between the whole and its parts, Philoponos deals with the relationship between the common and universal Logos of the nature of mankind (d-ꜥl gônyôt ̓ w-kôlnyôt ̓ d-kyn ̓ d-brnš ̓ mlt ̓ hy; "the commonality and the universality of the nature that belongs to the logos of man")[10] and its actual existence in individual and many men. He employs for this a number of analogies: the shipbuilder exists in many ships, the theory of the teacher in many students, the seal of the signet ring in many impressions. The point he wishes to make is that we conceive the universal rationality of a given thing on one level of reality as a whole which exists in and of itself, while on another level of reality it exists as that which is many and distinctly individual parts.

> " brnš ̓ gyr gôny ̓ bnynš ̓ sgy ̓ ̓ ḥd ̓ytyhôn. w-ꜣlp ̓ sby ̓ ̓ ḥd ̓.w-ydꜥt ̓
> dyn b-h b-dmôt ̓ w-ṯbꜥ ̓ dyn b-hy d-hy kd hy d-dmôt ̓ ḥd ̓ytyhôn"
> --"For many men are common as one and many ships are one and it is evident in the same sense the seals are likewise one."[11]

The significance of this conception is then found in chapter seven of *The Arbiter*. Philoponos explains in this chapter the way in which the terms "nature" (φύσις, natura, kyn ̓), "hypostasis" (ὑπόστασις, hypostasus, qnôm ̓), and "person" (πρόσωπον, persona, prṣôp ̓) are employed by the Church. In his explanation, there is explicated a dynamic relational complexity between the significations of the terms. They are to be related to one another in the same senses that the whole and the parts could be conceived as related together in chapter four.[12] This is to assert that the being or essence (οὐσία, essentia,

12

ᵓôsyᵓ) of the common logos of mankind possesses a nature which exists in the hypostatic reality of the individual person of the species. Because of the dynamics of this relational thought, Philoponos is able to assert about the term "nature" that it must be able to refer dynamically to two different levels of the same reality. On the one hand, "nature" refers to "being" or "essence" and is entailed by the existence of being or essence. On the other hand, "nature" must be able to refer to the "hypostasis" of an individual reality, a particular and differentiated existence in a hierarchy of reality. Thus he writes:[13]

"m-dyn klḥd mn kynᵓ lô l-ḥôdᵓytᵓ mtᵓmr hô mdm d-ᵓytôhy ᵓlᵓ trynᵓyt"
"Therefore, every one of the natures is not thought to signify one thing, but two." The concrete 'nature' of the particular is to understood in relation with the 'nature' of God. That is, in common with the way Severus of Antioch employed the term 'nature', the Grammarian asserts it must be able to refer at once both to the being of a thing (ᵓôsyᵓ) and its hypostatic reality (qnômᵓ), in the case of mankind his common logos (mltᵓ) and individual person (prṣôpᵓ). The necessity for this kind of dynamical thought is asserted by reference to the way the Church thought together the being and nature of the One Triune God in the hypostases or persons of God the Father, God the Son, and God the Holy Ghost.[14] Claiming that only the hypostasis of God the Son, the Eternal Word, became incarnate as Christ, Philoponos goes on to explain the union of the divine and human natures of Christ, which he believes belongs to the tradition of Cyril of Alexandria. He therefore affirms:[15]

bdgon w-ḥd kynᵓ d-mltᵓ ᵓlhᵓ d-mbsr môdynn w-b-hy d-môysp̄ ynn dylh d-ᵓlhᵓ mltᵓ. glylyt prṧynn l-h mn ᵓb̠ᵓ kyt w-rôhᵓ qdyṧᵓ --"So then we also confess one nature of the Word God become flesh and in that we add 'the Word God Himself, clearly, we distinguish him

13

(his nature) from the Father and the Holy Spirit."

The nature of the Son, the Word become flesh, must be at once both a particular man and yet as such able to refer to the Being of God as that Word the wholeness of which uniquely refers us to the Trinity of God. Philoponos goes on in the chapter to deny Nestorianism, identifying his thought completely with Cyril, and then to attempt to explicate the dynamics involved in asserting the one incarnate nature of Christ, one in which there never was a time when the human nature of Christ existed independently of the divine nature, a human nature which is what it is by its participation in the divine nature of Christ, the Word God. Philoponos believes his explanation is not only in line with Cyril and Severus, but is also rightly informed by the science that prevails at the Academy at Alexandria. He acknowledges that the use of such terms "nature," "hypostasis," and "person" are analogous to the manner of the "Peripetos" (περιπάτου--to the peripatetics), whose Porphyrian Tree was famous as a means to categorize and distinguish levels of reality at the school.[16] Nature was the rational participation in the Being or Essence of a genus as well as that which participated in the species of that genus as a more particular nature, so that the nature of species would always differentiate it from another species entailed in the same genus. It is evident that Philoponos is deeply influenced in his argument by the Episcopate Tradition of Alexandria as well as his training at the Academy. His effort to relate his scientific understanding of the cosmos to his theological understanding of God in Christ in such a way that they reinforce one another in a wholeness of truth which is from God is the ground upon which he built up his thought. John of Damascus took its anti-Chalcedon perspective as one which destroyed the mystery of Incarnation, rightfully identifying Philoponos with the thought of Severus of Antioch and affirming the findings of the Sixth Ecumenical Council. The dynamics of the thought of John Philoponos were not intelligible to the culmination of Eastern Orthodoxy nor to the West. The Word of God may become the person of Christ, but not as one nature. Nature and person could not be identified with one another. Thus, the divine nature could not suffer and must remain distinct in the person of Christ.[17]

But objection to the thought of Philoponos did not wait until the Anathema of 680 AD. There was evidently immediate criticism which brought him condemnation among the Eastern Orthodox. There are two responses to refutations of *The Arbiter* among the Sanda edition of the *Opuscula Monophysitica*,[18] and in his letter to Justinian, Philoponos is found defending for his Emperor the heart of the matter once again.[19] After paying due honor to the majesty of his king, John confesses the Rule of Faith while proclaiming the Emperor as the supreme guardian of all that is Christendom. He then acknowledges the debate between those who affirm that two natures belong to Christ and those, like himself, who would argue for one nature, that is one incarnate nature of Christ, a composite reality. He defends this nature, which is to be conceived according to the hypostatic union, against Nestorius and his followers, and then asserts the composition of the reality of Christ must be thought together in a way similar to Trinitarian thought, where the homoousios of Nicea is thought together with the hypostatic union of the divine and human natures, consistently and without confusion or contradiction. He argues that, since it was only the hypostatic reality of God the Son, the Eternal Word, which became flesh, and not the whole of the Trinity, therefore the human nature was assumed in such a way that it also is homoousia with the Father and the Spirit. Philoponos pretends an antagonist for this assertion and admits his objection is well founded. The whole thing is absolutely impossible, he exclaims, but nevertheless it is true for those who believe.[20] It can be and is to be explained only in the light of the revelation of God. This human nature possesses hypostatic reality in the hypostasic reality of the Word and is therefore homoousios with the Being of God, even though distinctly differentiated. There never was a time when there existed any other flesh except the humanity of the Lord assumed by the being of the Word of God. 'The Word become flesh' means a flesh has been 'fitted' to the Eternal Word. There is and can be no such thing as the humanity of Christ existing separately from God the Son, for if there could be, then some form of Nestorianism would be in order. But Nestorius was clearly anathematized at the Fourth Ecumenical Council of the Church.

Philoponos suggests the problem might be resolved by a proper consideration of the relationship between the whole and the parts. He employs analogies with the parts of man and man himself, and between the parts of a house and the house itself, and with the parts of a statue and the statue itself. None of these may be understood properly except as unique and dynamic realities made up of relations an integrity of which must exist between the whole that each thing is in itself and the realities of its parts. So the soul and body of a man form a whole identical in space with its parts, whose places are not separate from the whole man. So Christ must subsist as a unique and dynamic reality of the Word God in the world. Philoponos suggests that the phrases "in two natures" and "out of two natures," at the heart of the debate, are both capable of reference to the one reality of Christ, but "in two natures" is more easily misunderstood in the manner of the Nestorians and therefore the phrase "out of two natures" is best employed. "In two natures" can give the impression that the one reality can be divided up into individual parts capable of being numbered without reference to the one reality Christ is, which thought should not be entertained. "Out of two natures" is the phrase that best defends against the adoptionistic errors of Nestorius, who indeed was rightly declared Anathema by the Empire of Justinian.

In the East, the debate over the thought of Philoponos is carried on by the clash between Peter of Callinicum and Damian of Alexandria in the final decades of the sixth century.[21] Both of these orthodox patriarchs considered that the Christological thought of John Philoponos had led him inevitably into a form of "tritheism." They considered that his concrete Christ as an individual reality was different from God. But in their efforts to explain the causes of the inevitability of this conclusion about the Grammarian's argument, they were forced into accusing one another of different heresies. Peter thought Damian to be Sabellian in his argument against Philoponos, and Damian came to consider that Peter had a tendency towards the very "tritheism" for which he claimed to condemn the Grammarian, towards a reductionism, as we might speak of it today. The exchange is, I think, instructive. Philoponos had claimed that the one incarnate nature out of the two natures of the person of Christ could not be grasped by the senses alone, but could only be understood as one reality by the mind in a theory shaped by the invisible dimension of the nature.[22] Neither Peter nor Damian wished to be identified with Philoponos in this assertion. Both of them thought this must mean that Philoponos was a nominalist thereby, and in such a manner that the hypostatic realities of the three persons of the Trinity were one, not in reality, but existed only in the mind of the believer. The attention paid to Philoponos by Leontius of Byzantium records the error as one made in concert with Aristotle.[23] Ebied, Van Roey, and Wickham have recognized that this was not the intention of Philoponos.[24] But they agree finally with Peter and Damian that he is ultimately a nominalist.[25] To them, the unity of the consubstantial nature of the hypostatic realities of the persons of the Godhead exists for the Grammarian not as an objective reality outside of the mind of the believer, but is only a construct of that mind.

17

Perhaps it will be helpful to look more closely into the debate between Peter and Damian. In his letter to the Patriarch of Alexandria, Peter berates the Alexandrian scientist, quoting from a work Philoponos wrote *Against Themistius*, for thinking the being or <u>essence</u> (ʾôsyʾ) of the Divine Trinity as existing only in the mind of the believer and not in reality (b-sôʿryʾ).[26] Philoponos had affirmed that the consubstantiality of the natures (kynʾ šôy b-ʾôsyʾ) of the persons of the Godhead existed as <u>hypostatic</u> realities with individual properties (dylytʾ myqnnytʾ d-qnômʾ) in a community with the divine nature. He had used as an analogy the concept of mankind, where the race exists as a community of individuals in the mind of the observer only. One never experiences mankind with the senses, but only Peter or Paul, etc. That is, one man may die but mankind does not. Peter uses the comparison to affirm that Philoponos denies the real existence of the Oneness of God. With him, Damian agrees. But when they attempt to think through with one another just how being or essence should be related to the hypostatic realities of the persons of God, they find themselves at odds. Evidently, even Philoponos, with Peter and Damian, wanted to confess the <u>homoousion</u> which the Church had inherited from Nicea. But Peter agreed with Philoponos that the hypostatic realities of the persons of the Trinity existed as consubstantial realities, which are differentiated by individual properties (the Father alone begets, the Son alone is begotten, and the Spirit alone proceeds), in the one Godhead. Damian evidently took this agreement to mean that Peter was also a tritheist, providing Peter the reason for his letter to Damian. How could Peter think the nature of the being of God existed as three natures with <u>individual properties</u> in the <u>hypostatic realities</u> of the persons of the Trinity without confessing essentially three gods? Peter's defense, wishing to distinguish himself from the nominalism of Philoponos, contends that Damian's failure to understand the nature of the persons in the Godhead makes him li-

18

able to a modalism of one kind or another and accuses his accuser of Sabellianism. That is, Damian fails to grasp the hypostatic realities of the persons in their real differentiated natures. Peter thought Damian's error was in the confusion of the individual properties of the hypostases with the hypostases themselves.[27] For Damian, as for many Orthodox thinkers in this debate, the nature of the being or essence of God could in no way be identified with the hypostases or persons of the Godhead, for such an assertion led inevitably into tritheism, a claim John of Damascus later affirmed.[28] For Peter, this did not understand properly Nicea's homoousion, where the Son and the Spirit were proclaimed to be equal in being to God the Father, and this leads inevitably to a devaluation of the real meaning of persons in the Godhead.

The debate led the two patriarchs into deeper and more emotional conflict until they regarded each other as enemies. Being able to declare together an Anathema upon the thought of John Philoponos did not provide for them the kind of ground upon which they could resolve the problems of relating the concepts of being, nature, hypostasis, and person as they are to be employed when attempting to refer with our minds to the mystery of the reality of the revelation of God in Christ. When it comes to the complexities of thought thrust upon us by this revelation of God, agreement that another is anathema to the salvific truth of that reality does not guarantee agreement in an effort to say what is properly to be apprehended of its truth. It seems Peter and Damian learned this lesson the hard way, and at the expense of their friendship.[29]

But our purpose here is to show how so-called "Monophysites" condemned by the West's development of the assertions of Chalcedon, could condemn one of their own and surround the thought of the Alexandrian scientist with one form of anathema or another. In the West, John Philoponos was seen as a Monophysite. In the East, among Monophysites the Grammarian was seen as a tritheist. It is the popular perception of textbook histories that Monophysites did not believe in the humanity of Christ. It is the popular perception of many Orthodox that Philoponos made too concrete the person of Jesus Christ. That such contradictory condemnations can be applied to the thought of one man should, perhaps, give us reason to suspect the blanket of anathemas with which his work has come to be covered. The historical fact is that the anathemas of John Philoponos have effectively rendered his thought and work absolutely obscure to the Church, both in the West and East.

The Greek originals of *The Arbiter* were destroyed. Ebied, Van Roey, and Wickham claim there was made by the Monophysite Church an effort to curtail even the Syriac translations of the works of the Grammarian.[30] However, Wright notes that *The Arbiter* became a part of the curriculum in the schools of Edessa and the Persian Empire.[31] Perhaps it was from these centers that there survived in Estrangela translations of *The Arbiter* which have been preserved in the Vatican library.[32] Vööbus has pointed out that John Philoponos had dedicated his work to Jaqob Burdana, the Father of the Monophysite Church in the midst of its persecution in the sixth century.[33] Outside of the authority of the Imperial Sees, it is easy to understand their preservation, but I have read no comment on how they came to the Vatican. In 1930, Šanda provided an edition of *The Arbiter*, now in the British Museum, with a translation into Latin.[34] In the same year, Hermann attempted an analysis of the work, recognizing the Grammarian's use of the crucial terms from his Aristotelian and Christian background.[35] He is able to understand that, though Philoponos may have learned from Aristotle, he is free to argue against the master, and that the Alexandrian scientist in *The Arbiter* is attempting to argue in a cool and calm spirit for the confession of Cyril of Alexandria against Nestorian efforts to interpret the Person of Christ,[36] something he thought was very possible if the Church confessed "of two natures" rather than "in two natures" to the hypostasis of Christ.[37] Hermann agrees with Damian before him that it was the identification of "nature" with the "hypostasis" or "person" which led Philoponos inevitably into Tritheism.[38] Although Hermann appreciates the dynamic effort made by the scientist to understand the union of the natures of Christ, he cannot accept the claim that the union is apprehended properly in the argument. The hypostatic union of Cyril's Confessions grasped only in Θεώρια is not acceptable. However well the scientist has argued, he remains for Hermann the anathematized Monophysite.[39] Nature may not be identified with hypostasis or person when confessing Christ.

It is this kind of evaluation which one finds throughout the encyclopaedic literature on John Philoponos. The most thorough general introductions to Philoponos have appeared with Güdeman's article in *Paulys Real-Encyclopädie* and with Bardy's in the *Dictionnaire de Theologie Catholique*.[40] Güdeman believed the Anathema of Philoponos began when the scientist failed to appear before an Egyptian Synod.[41] *The Arbiter* (Schiedsrichter) is known as a work of seven chapters rather than the ten chapters later found by Hermann. For Güdeman, the Alexandrian scientist, born in Caesarea around 490, was converted to Christianity while a student under Ammonius at the Academy under the influence of the Episcopate of Alexandria about 520 AD.[42] The efforts at the Academy to synthesize the Platonic and Aristotelian traditions provided the Grammarian with a broad range of concerns. The work touches upon philosophical, grammatical, and theological fields of study and discusses everything from pure logic and the physical sciences to linguistic and finally theological science. Güdeman's evaluation of *The Arbiter* is much the same as

Hermann's later conclusion. "Es handelt sich um die Verteidigung des Mono-physitimus und Begründung des Tritheität."[43] He also writes concerning the relation of the work to Aristotelian Science:[44]

Somit werden wir auch Werke, wie περὶ κοσμοποιάς und Διαιτητής, in denen er als erster den für die Kulturgeschichte des Abendlandes so folgenschweren Schritt tat, die aristotelische mit der Christlichen Lehre in Einklang zu brin-gen, in eine frühere Periode seiner theologischen Schriftstellertätigkeit set-zen müssen.

Both of these assertions are readily passed on by subsequent scholars. Bardy quotes Leontius of Byzantium and his argument with Philoponos about the identification of "nature" with "hypostasis" or "person." The Church claims this must mean that there are three divine natures in the Trinity which is condemned at Nicea. But Philoponos, referring to the Aristotelian categories of individuals (ἄτομα) and particular substances (μερικάι οὐσία), in-sists there are three natures with <u>particular substances</u> existing with the hypostases or persons that are "une οὐσία commune."[45] Bardy then con-cludes, referring to the doctrines of Philoponos:[46]

> Elle ne tarda pas à devenir pour les hérésioloques, un
> simple objet de curiosité.

It is not as if, through all the curiosity, there was merely negative evaluation and interpretation of the doctrines. As early as 1856 Herzog, when he noticed that the earlier impression given by a reference to Sergius in the work of Philoponos on the creation of the world (Phot. Bibl. codex 240) was in error, could write positively about the Alexandrian:[47]

> Philoponus folgte nämlich in christologischen Streit der
> Egyptischen Partei, er war Monophysit und als Philosoph
> vorwiegend Aristoteliker, so auffallend es auch erscheinen mag,
> dass in demselben Manne eine mystische Richtung mit einer rein
> verständigen, treuneden Dialektik in Berührung trat.

His analysis of the thought displays some sympathy with it and knows that the accusations of Tritheism cannot mean that Philoponos really wanted to worship three gods. But he writes finally that the Grammarian introduced a kind of dangerous thinking into the dogmatic efforts of the Church which allowed the beginning of the nominalism of the Scholastics.[48]

A survey of patristic commentators on the matter and the encyclopedic literature reveals that, in spite of occasional efforts to penetrate further into the problem of "nature" and "hypostasis" found in the works of Philoponos, the Anathema of the Grammarian evidently remains effective. Even before Hermann's study, Lebon had argued that Monophysites like Severus of Antioch were not Monophysites in a heretical sense.[49] They were more concerned about interpreting properly the tradition of the thought of Cyril of Alexandria than anything else, and argued against any Apollinarian tendency in the Eastern Church of Justinian's Empire. But this effort seems to have made no compelling impression upon modern scholarship. We seem to pass on, without actually reading the extant texts, the evaluations of the earlier interpreters.

Harnack, arguing that the Creeds of Christendom represented the successful influence of Hellenism upon the Church, understands the identification made by Philoponos of "nature" with "hypostasis" as the source of his Monophysite tritheism.[50] The identification is the result of an Aristotelian conception which the scientist attempted to harmonize with Church Doctrine. He states that "... we gather that John spoke of τρεῖς μερικαὶ οὐσίαι and accepted the notion of the οὐσία κοινή which, however, exists only in conception."[51] He thinks the boldness with which Philoponos defended the Monophysites against the Chalcedonian Creed is testimony to the freedom displayed in the East in the face of tradition and the imposition of a foreign power,[52] an argument not consistent with the assertion that John was a

23

thoroughgoing Aristotelian. In spite of the greatness of Philoponos as a scientist, his contribution to dogma and heresy could only serve as a foil against which the Scholasticism of the Middle Ages could evolve its <u>via media</u> between Aristotle and the Grammarian.[53] Since, of course, the synthesis in the Middle Ages of Aristotle and Church Dogma had to be dismantled in the light of the modern world, yet again Philoponos' thought appears as a curiosity of curiosities.

A similar assessment of John Philoponos is made by Prestige.[54] Referring to the observations of Leontius of Byzantium and John of Damascus, John is understood as a moderate Monophysite who, in defending the Cyrillian Christology of Alexandria's Episcopate, attempted as a scientist "to reach the concrete."[55] Philoponos had defined "nature" in both a generic sense and a particular sense, according to Aristotelian categories, where the generic sense is considered an abstraction existing in the mind only and the particular sense embodies the only real existence of the generic nature. Adopting this way of thinking, Philoponos is led to confess three "natures" in the Godhead and his heresy. Prestige writes:[56]

> But it is easy to see that if he had grasped the truth of the single identical concrete ousia of God, instead of understanding the common essence of the godhead in an abstract sense, he might have found that the concrete physis which he desiderated was embodied in that ousia, without triplicating a distinct physis in each of the three hypostaseis.

It is interesting that Prestige considers John's efforts to be both like Nestorianism and like the Cappadocian need to defend itself against charges of tritheism.

Altaner lists, then, John Philoponos (a "lover of work") as one who was anxious to reconcile the teaching of the Church with Aristotelianism.[57] *The Arbiter* (The Umpire) represents a tritheism which admits only a notion-al unity of the three Persons of the Godhead. Altaner rightly claims that the Alexandrian scientist had as his mentor in Christology Severus of Antioch, the greatest Monophysite theologian in the East in the early sixth century. One doubts, however, Severus and later Philoponos were ever anxious for the Aristotelian synthesis. The basis of their beginnings lay elsewhere.

Henry Chadwick implies that the leadership of the Academy of Alexandria fell to Philoponos about the time Justinian closed the Academy of Athens in 529 AD.[58] He recognizes Philoponos' struggle to assert a spherical earth against the literal understandings of the Bible rendered by Cosmas Indicopleustes, and mentions his deduction, against pagan belief in a Ptolemaic universe, that the heavens could not be divine and contained fiery objects whose physics and chemistry were the same as earth's.[59] But in spite of his brilliance in these areas, Chadwick continues the ban on the concreteness for which the scientist sought. The Alexandrian Grammarian must be considered a nominalist and Monophysite.

In his work on Boethius, Chadwick reaffirms the significance of the scientific work of Philoponos and appreciates the success of his attack on Proclus, the teacher of Ammonius Hermais, who was the teacher of Philoponos at the Academy.[60] One cannot deny the profound grasp the Grammarian had upon the scientific issues of his day.[61] He compares the contribution of Philoponos to the ill-fated Boethius, claiming that, even if we do not admit they were once fellow students of the Porphyrian Tree under Ammonius, we must understand their academic backgrounds to be deeply related in the Neoplatonic traditions which characterized the schools of their day. They are both genuine scientists or philosophers who attempted to contribute to the Christendom of Justinian's Empire.[62]

In the fourth chapter of his study of Boethius, Chadwick wrestles with the Christian dogmatics of the Latin philosopher. He describes how Boethius learned of the urgency of the Christological debate in the East when he heard Scythian monks plead in Rome for a positive response which they might use to explain a via media in the controversy evidently raging throughout the Empire over the union of the divine and human natures of Christ. Astonished by the undisciplined manner in which the debate took place among the senators and churchmen of Rome, Boethius decided to set himself the task of writing a statement whose clarity and definition might contribute to the kind of reconciliation for which the monks sought. We must look more closely at this chapter when we consider specifically the scientific tradition which was the Academy of Alexandria. We will gain much insight into the issues surrounding the writing of *The Arbiter*, since it appears to be evident that John Philoponos was asked by Justinian to do in the East what Boethius attempted in Rome. Suffice it to say here that there is nothing in Chadwick's effort that would compel us to contradict the force of the Anathema on Philoponos. He sees the Grammarian as a follower of Severus of Antioch who opposes with superb arguments the Chalcedonians. *The Arbiter* is a cool analysis whose intention is to find a via media in their debate. As a scientist in the Neoplatonic tradition, John thought that to describe the union of the divine and human natures of Christ the phrase "in two natures" was undesirable because it allowed one to speak of the reality of Christ as if there was an issue of numbering, an arithmetic whose logic could be imposed upon the "single composite nature" of the being of our Lord and Savior, which is grounded in mystery. It introduced into the language about the incarnation a question of parts which was not appropriate to its reality. It allowed a Nestorian interpretation of it which was against the Confession and Rule of Faith with the Church. But Philoponos' preference for the phrase "of two natures" has behind it an effort to explain the Divine Mystery by concepts which originated in the science of his time and drove the scientist with his genius into the nominalism and Monophysitism of which he has been accused. Chadwick allows, I believe, that the consensus of opinion about the tritheism of Philoponos should not be understood to mean that his intention was to worship three gods. But the effort of the Grammarian to relate faith and reason has surely led the scientist to think he knows more than he really does.[63]

Again, Wallace-Hadrill records the whole effort as a "curious theological disturbance which... denied the Trinity altogether."[64] But the considerable confusion in his analysis of the disturbance is cogent. Mistaking a Grammarian by the name of John for John Philoponos, Wallace-Hadrill proceeds to understand the thought of Philoponos in light of the defense made by Severus of Antioch against John the Grammarian.[65] He actually uses the thought of John the Grammarian, who wrote in defense of Chalcedon, as the thought of John Philoponos, who never wrote in defense of Chalcedon. In this way, he shows that Philoponos' use of the crucial terms in the controversy, especially the identification of "nature" with "hypostasis," is thoroughly Aristotelian and reductionistic. He shows how the Grammarian identifies nature and hypostasis with the categories of Aristotle where nature is a genus of a species and a secondary substance, one which, although not strictly only a quality or attribute of a thing, does not exist in itself and is not a primary substance. Against this reductionism, argues Wallace- Hadrill, was Severus of Antioch. Severus argues that we should begin with the unity of God and therefore the structure of the Trinity does not mean He is not One, and we cannot think from the particulars to the whole, whose reality we must admit.[66] Wallace-Hadrill then contends that Severus taught Philoponos his expertise with Aristotelian categories. But we have already seen that Severus was in fact a spiritual father to Philoponos, whose thought follows his mentor here and not the reductionist analysis of John the Grammarian. It is with this kind of confusion behind him that Wallace-Hadrill can write:[67]

> It is not Arianism, but it is clear why the sixth century theologians who still adhered to the Nicene definition should be able to brand as Arians the grammarian and his followers such as Conon and Eugenius.

He then goes on to acknowledge the action on the part of the contemporaries of Philoponos who saw to it that his work was anathematized in both Alexandria and Constantinople.

W. H. C. Frend has made perhaps the most complete study of the Monophysite movement in the Church, and credits Philoponos with an independence of mind that is able to stand against any notion that the Emperor was <u>the</u> image of God, and for a government which rested upon the free will of the governed.[68] But the only attention he gives Philoponos in his study, whom he recognizes as a zealot and a great intellect of the Christian faith, and not simply a lover of work, refers at last to Hermann's article and affirms John's tritheism, the result once again of identifying "nature" with "hypostasis" or "person" so that, in his tremendous achievement in his work on *The Rise of Christianity*, there is no mention of Philoponos.[69]

This catena of judgments could be multiplied. Everywhere that one might look for reference to Philoponos one finds his condemnation.[70] All of the encyclopedic literature will picture Philoponos in some sense or another as a Monophysitic tritheist. *The Cambridge Histories* treat Philoponos as such,[71] so that it is little wonder that modern philosophers and scientists, interested mainly in the scientific works of Philoponos, have little concern for the theology of the Grammarian and simply pass on the Anathema with the consensus of theologians and historians of the Church. His science, the implication always is, does not stem from Orthodox Christianity. Shmuel Sambursky, writing in *The Encyclopedia of Philosophy*, while extolling the genius of Philoponos, can devote one sentence to the theological works of the Alexandrian scientist:[72]

> He was, probably from birth, a Christian who adhered to the Monophysite sect, which was declared heretical in the seventh century.

Over against this relentless and continuous catena of judgments in the consensus of opinion concerning the condemnation of John Philoponos, stands the regard of the Edinburgh theologian, Thomas Torrance. As early as 1969, Torrance began pointing to Philoponos as a scientist who had rejected, because of his belief in God, certain fundamental concepts associated with Aristotelian ideas of space and time and the physics of the world.[73] The Alexandrian scientist, following the perspective on the relation between God and cosmos established by the Fathers of the Church, developed relational views of space and time which enable him to advance the development of thought in ancient science beyond his contemporaries, a development that found no echo among his contemporaries.[74] Philoponos actually contemplated a reconstruction of the foundations of knowledge in such a startling way that he displayed "remarkable anticipations of twentieth century scientific thought."[75] In an article first published in 1976, and now reprinted in his recent book, *Transformation and Convergence in the Frame of Knowledge,* Torrance suggests that it was the classical patristic theology of God as light which provided the ground upon which the Grammarian attempted to build his physics of light.[76] It was the incarnation and the doctrine of creation thought together realistically that compelled his thought in such a manner as to provide a solid and serious view of the mystery of God with us, with the matter in the world where an appropriate rationality towards them needs to be apprehended.[77] It was this development of thought which provided the basis for the scientist's effort in theology. Torrance has written:[78]

> For John Philoponos, however, who did not think in an Aristotelian way, in line with the theological way, in line with the theological and scientific tradition to which he belonged, nature meant "reality," so that for him to think of Christ as "one nature" meant that he was "one reality," not a schizoid being. John Philoponus was no monophysite in the heretical sense, but the accusation of heresy had the effect of denigrating also his antidualist thought in science and philosophy. This represents, in my view, one of the greatest tragedies in the history of science as well as theology for it really means the Church was ultimately unwilling to work out in the rigorous way required the distinctly Christian ideas of the relation between God and the world.

It is claimed that the tendency in the race to think away the real contingent rationality and nature of created reality produces those categories of thought against which Philoponos so ingeniously struggled.[79] Far from it being true that the scientific thought of John Philoponos led him to theological heresy, Torrance claims that his concerns with the relation of God as uncreated light and the created light of the cosmos, as he found it in the Church Fathers, allowed him to make effective use of analogies seeking to point to the divine light in the incarnation of God's eternal Logos in Jesus Christ.[80] And most recently, reporting on a conference held at the Institute of Classical Studies in London, Torrance has called for the Church to begin to re-evaluate the theology of John Philoponos in the way that the scientific community is now seeking to do with the thought of the physicist of Alexandria.[81]

Although the opposition to these claims of Torrance is singular in the consensus of opinion on Philoponos among Western scholars, there exists resonance with him among the Orthodox of the Eastern Church. Recently, because of Ecumenical movements in the Church attempting to understand anew the schisms which have historically existed between East and West, Archbishop Methodios Fouyas, discussing the use of the term nature by the Councils of the Church, could write finally:[82]

> Problems such as these have continued in the difference between the so-called Eastern "monophysites" and the "Chalcedonians" who, as far as I can see, basically intend the same thing.

In this evaluation, the Archbishop claims that we must distinguish between theologians like Severus of Antioch and John Philoponos, who ought not to be confused with Apollinarian and Eutychian Monophysites.[83] With this in mind, he thinks, it would be possible to reach some statement of the Person of Jesus Christ upon which both East and West might agree. If the Church be but willing to do the kind of disciplined thinking which one can call "scientific theology," then real progress could be made in the way that the Rule of Faith points all of its members to a reality, upon which we will be able to agree, which is the saving grace of God in the Lord and Savior of all things, of creation and of the Church. Harnack perceived that the Severian Monophysites "did not in any way shrink from contact with the great spiritual forces of the time."[84] Joannou has sought to appreciate the contribution of Philoponos as the first Christian to attempt an explication of a philosophical system in the pagan world.[85] It seems difficult to show that the Alexandrian scientist actually intended to worship three gods or deny Christ as the God who reigned even above his Emperor in the Christendom of the Justinian Empire. R. K. Sorabji has written:[86]

> Philoponus has not always got the credit he deserves, partly because of the Anathema which was imposed on him in AD 680, just over a hundred years after his death.

Another part of the reason must be the way the consensus of scholarship in the West has passed on the judgment of that Anathema. Can we with Torrance, and the glimpses a few others have given us into the thought of the Grammarian, begin to appreciate afresh the contribution he sought to make

31

to the Church and the scientific culture of his generation? Would such an appreciation not help us in our time to understand better the way we are called to witness to the Word of God in our theological and scientific enterprizes? Is it not, after all, true that every theology is shaped by its view of the world where we have our being, that our freedom to follow our God is formed by our ability to hear in this world a call that only He can make upon human life?

Before leaving this chapter on the Anathema of John Philoponos, I think it is, in conclusion, appropriate to say something about the tradition in the Church of the Anathema itself. For the modern mind, it is difficult to understand the manner in which evidently sincere and ardent believers in Jesus Christ could attempt to create a Rule of Faith in such a way that they could proceed to make of once close friends the most bitter of enemies, and do so over discussions in which the difference between an "in" and an "of" could spell the difference between acceptance and rejection into communion with the fellowship of the saints of God. We grow easily skeptical of the value of such enterprises and tend to shy away from the disciplines. Is it not better to drop the whole of the matter and simply love one another?[87]

But then we must realize that love may not be divorced from truth, our passions from our minds, and we discover all over again that we must, if we truly believe, seek to understand the God who has made things the way things have been made to be. That is the real value of the Anathema. Torrance, with most scholars I believe, would have us to understand the Anathema as the attempt of the Church to mark out the "boundaries" of a confession the substance and essence of which is nothing less or more than the salvation God has given us.[88] Outside these "boundaries" exists by the nature of the case what is not true or love, but what is false and hateful, hateful to a holy God who is an enemy of evil. The Anathema, grounded in the

32

biblical traditions, would root out of the world that God has made for Himself every kind of evil and delusion. In this light, it is an essential part of our effort as the Church to follow the Creator and Redeemer.[89] It is a word that says to the world there is a judgment of God and, unless we will allow such judgment, we will never know real love or truthful truth. That we can take this tradition and with it hear another word besides the Word of God and create not "boundaries" but all sorts and kinds of legalisms suffocating the human spirit means that we can with our freedom abuse the gift we have been given. But this possibility, a danger whose potential has been realized in every generation of the history of our race, does not mean we may abolish the Anathema from our midst. It is better that, over the centuries, John Philoponos could be wrongly condemned than that the Church should think that she has no real authority with the God of all truth and love in the world. The Church, better than any structure among the institutions of this world, knows the meaning of forgiveness. She has always before her the God of all creation, whose death upon a cross continues to teach, from the impossible possibility of the perspective of His ascended life, the meaning and significance of forgiveness. She knows no other purpose but that which is seen in the light of this forgiveness. To abolish the Anathema would be to remain ignorant of this impossible possibility, and to forsake the ancient traditions which have handed down the communion of the divine love and eternal life of the truth in God.

NOTES TO CHAPTER ONE

1. H. R. Percival, *The Seven Ecumenical Councils,* vol. XIV, Library of Nicene and Post-Nicene Fathers, Grand Rapids: Eerdmans, 1971, pp. 324-53.

2. Adolf Harnack, *History of Dogma*, vol. V, New York: Dover Publications, 1961, p. 278, observes the schisms in the Church caused by the controversies were never actually ended by the Council.

3. W. H. C. Frend, *The Rise of the Monophysite Movement*, Cambridge: Cambridge University Press, 1972, pp. 201-20. Frend's assertion that there was in the West no Chalcedonian theologian who can be compared with Severus is important. He must have been a major force in the Episcopate of Alexandria during his life and a great influence upon John Philoponos there.

4. Ibid., *Saints and Sinners in the Early Church*, Wilmington: Michael Glazier, 1985, pp. 157-73. This is perhaps the best recent, concise rendering of the life and significance of Severus.

5. R. Graffin and F. Nau, "Letters of Severus," Patrologia Orientalis, vol. 14 (nos. 67-71), ed. and trans. F. W. Brooks, Belgique, 1973, pp. 28-29.

6. See the "Letter to Eupraxius," pp. 6-69, for the complete discussion. This thought is best understood as an effort to explicate the concepts of perichoresis and coinherence implied by the confession of the homoousion and hypostatic union which Severus had inherited from Nicene theology.

7. St. John of Damascus, *Writings,* vol. 37, Fathers of the Church, trans. F. H. Chase, Jr., New York, 1958, pp. xxx-xxxi. Cf. also, Leontii Byzantini, *Patrologiae Cursus Completus*, Series Graeca, 86, 2, ed. J. P. Migne, Paris, 1865, col. 1769-1900. See, De Sectis, 5.6.

8. Ibid., pp. 138-39.

9. Ibid., pp. 140-48, Migne, PG, 94.743-754, and A. Šanda, *The Arbiter*, pp. 17, 20-24.

10. Because part of the purpose for my dissertation is a call for a fresh translation and interpretation of *The Arbiter*, I will be referring the reader to the extant Syriac Texts edited by Šanda, p. 17, lines 9-10.

11. Ibid., p. 17, lines 17-19. Logically, this asserts the proposition that the whole may not be related to the sum and the parts in the same way that the sum and the parts are related to one another. This kind of dynamical thought provides that kind of unique necessity which obtains for the whole and its parts which are not distinguished in space.

12. Ibid., p. 21, section 22, lines 1-4.

13. Ibid., line 9.

14. Ibid., p. 22, section 23, lines 1-5.

15. Ibid., lines 15-17.

16. See Eleonore Stump, *Boethius' De topicis differentis*, Ithaca: Cornell University Press, 1978, pp. 235-246 for the use of the Tree.

17. G. W. Bromiley, *Historical Theology, An Introduction,* Grand Rapids: Eerdmans, 1978, pp. 147-55. Cf. also, T. F. Torrance, "The Place of Christology in Biblical and Dogmatic Theology," in *Theology in Reconstruction*, Eerdmans: Grand Rapids, 1965, pp. 128-49. See pages 131 and 149 especially for the way the Word is considered to entail the humanity of Christ. Obviously, the struggle to understand the relation continues.

18. A. Šanda, ed., *Opuscula Monophysitica Ioannis Philoponi*, Beryti Phoeniciorum, Typographia Catholica, PP. Soc. Jesu, 1930, pp. 63-94. The edition actually includes, besides the argument of *The Arbiter*, an epitome in which are gathered some main points in the argument, two responses to those who repudiated the argument, a homily on the interchange of the whole and part, and a letter to Justinian. The Vatican manuscript actually contains all this plus a letter to Sergius, a Patriarch contemporary to John Philoponos (Vaticanus syriacus 144).

19. Ibid., pp. 123-30. Because of its value for appreciating the life-setting of *The Arbiter* and because it has never been put into English, I will translate the complete letter in chapter four, where I will discuss the relation of this argument to the scientific tradition in which Philoponos labored. An appreciation of this letter will also provide evidence that John was not perceived by Justinian as merely an extension of the thought of Severus of Antioch.

20. Ibid., pp. 126-27. The dynamics of the thought of John Philoponos, following the scientific tradition in Alexandria, are not intelligible unless one allows various levels of reality to be related to each other by a creative and uniquely given rationality.

21. R. Y. Ebied, A. Van Roey, and L. R. Wickham, *Peter of Callinicum*, Leuven: Department Orientalistich, 1981.

22. Ibid., p. 26. Cf. "in theoria," of 'The Letter to Justinian'.

23. *Leontii Byzantini, Patrologiae Cursus Completus*, Series Graeca, 86.2, ed. J. P. Migne, Paris, 1865, 1233-34.

24. Ebied, et al., op. cit., p. 30.

25. Ibid., p. 31.

26. Ibid., p. 50.

27. Ibid., p. 34ff.

28. *John of Damascus*, op. cit., p. 139. The Damascene traced the heresy back to the immediate disagreement in the East with Leo's Tome at Chalcedon. He seems to see no problem in condemning Philoponos both as a Monophysite and Tritheist.

29. R. Y. Ebied, "Peter of Antioch and Damian of Alexandria: The End of a Friendship," in *A Tribute to Arthur Vööbus,* ed. R. H. Fischer, Lutheran

School of Theology at Chicago, 1977, pp. 277-82. The author contends we must understand the seriousness of the dispute. Salvation was believed to be at stake, the substance of real faith made the issue. Cf. Karl Barth, *Church Dogmatics*, vol. I.1, pp. 348-75 for the modern discussion of the problem. If I understand Barth correctly here, he would not require that Philoponos was a nominalist and may have been sympathetic with his effort.

30. R. Y. Ebied, et al., *Peter of Callinicum*, op. cit., p. 21ff.

31. W. Wright, *A Short History of Syriac Literature*, London: Adam and Charles Black, 1894, p. 24. It should be remembered, however, that Philoponos' works would have been disliked by Nestorian schools.

32. Vatican 144 folio I va-30va Assemani, Bibl. Vat. cod. manuscr. catalogus I 3 5. 250-52, 30vb-39vb, 38vb-45va, 45va-49vb.

33. A. Vööbus, "The Origin of the Monophysite Church in Syria and Mesopotamia," CH, p. 26, footnote 104. Although, W. Smith and H. Wace, in *A Dictionary of Christian Biography*, vol. III, London: John Murray, 1882, pp. 425-27, had claimed that Philoponos wrote *The Arbiter* (Διαιτητής) for Sergius of Antioch, but there is a tendency here and in the encyclopaedia literature to confuse Philoponos with a Grammarian who opposed Severus of Antioch, and this must be a mistake (cf. Th. Hermann, "Johannes Philoponus als Monophysit," ZNW 29 (1930), p. 209-10, and J. J. Herzog, *Real-Encyclopädie*, vol.6, p. 760).

34. A. Šanda, ed., *Opuscula Monophysitica*, BM. Syr. II 587, op. cit. I have obtained a copy of this edition from the British Museum and a copy of the Vatican Manuscript. There seems adequate material here for a text-critical study to be made, as well as an evaluation of the different form and content of the argument.

35. Th. Hermann, "Johannes Philoponus als Monophysit," ZNTW 29 (1930), pp. 209-64.

36. Ibid., pp. 239-40, 258.

37. Ibid., p. 243.

38. Ibid., p. 263.

39. Ibid., p. 264.

40. A. Güdeman, "Ioannes Philoponus, griechischer Grammatiker und Christlicher Theologe," *Paulys Real Encyclopädie*, ed. G. Wissowa and W. Kroll, Stuttgart, 1916, pp. 1764-95, and G. Bardy, "Jean Philopon," DTC, vol. 8, Paris, 1903ff., pp. 830-39.

41. Güdeman, p. 1766.

42. Ibid., p. 1769.

43. Ibid., p. 1791.

44. Ibid., p. 1770.

45. Bardy, op. cit., p. 838.

46. Ibid., p. 839.

47. J. J. Herzog, *Real Encyclopädie*, vol. 6, Stuttgart, 1856, p. 761. It is interesting to notice that, at this time, the Διαιτητής ἢ περὶ ἐνώσεως was still lost. The author lists the only extant texts as the excerpts in Leontius, De sectis, Act. 5, apud Galland XII, p. 641; John Damascene, De Laeres I, pp. 101-7; Niceph. Call., XVIII, p. 57; and Mansi, Council. XI, p. 301. Between 1856 and Sanda's work, manuscripts of The Arbiter were discovered.

48. Ibid., p. 761.

49. J. Lebon, *Le Monophysisme Severien,* Lovanii: Universitatis Catholicae Typographus, 1909.

50. A. Harnack, *History of Dogma*, 4 volumes, New York, Dover, 1961, vol. IV, p. 125.

51. Ibid., p. 125, footnote 1.

52. Op. cit., vol. V, p. 240.

53. Op. cit., vol. VII, p. 29 (for science, vol. III, p. 249).

54. G. L. Prestige, *God in Patristic Thought*, London: SPCK, 1952, pp. 282-84.

55. Ibid., p. 282.

56. Ibid., pp. 282-3.

57. B. Altaner, *Patrology*, trans. H. Graet, Freiburg, Herder, 1960, pp. 612-13.

58. H. Chadwick, *The Early Church*, New York: Penguin Books, 1981, p. 172.

59. Ibid., p. 207.

60. H. Chadwick, *Boethius*, Oxford: Clarendon Press, 1981, pp. 19-20.

61. Ibid., pp. 72, 106, 133, 147.

62. Ibid., p. 149.

63. Some of this impression I have received from personal communication with Professor Chadwick. The problem of space, place, and the incarnation is involved here.

64. D. S. Wallace-Hadrill, *Christian Antioch*, Cambridge: Cambridge University Press, 1982, pp. 93-95, 106-9.

65. Ibid., p. 95.

66. Severus teaches that the One Creator God is the Triune God in such a way that the three hypostases or persons are homoousia, with the result that we apprehend the nature of the Son as distinct. See E. W. Brooks, "A Collection of Letters of Severus of Antioch," PO, ed. R. Graffin and F. Nau, vol. 14, nos. 67-71, Editions Brepols, Belgique, 1973, pp. 9-13.

67. Wallace-Hadrill, op. cit., p. 94.

68. Frend, op. cit., p. 59.

69. W. H. C. Frend, *The Rise of Christianity*, Philadelphia: Fortress Press, 1984.

70. Cf. J. Tixeront, *History of Dogmas*, vol. III, Westminster, Maryland: Christian Classics, 1984 (1916), pp. 187-88. Also, J. L. Gonzalez, *A History of Christian Thought*, vol. II, Nashville: Abingdon Press, 1983, pp. 89ff.

71. A. H. Armstrong, *The Cambridge History of Later Greek and Early Medieval Philosophy,* Cambridge: Cambridge University Press, 1967, pp. 477-83.

72. S. Sambursky, *The Encyclopedia of Philosophy*, vol. 6, New York: MacMillan, 1967, p. 156.

73. T. F. Torrance, *Space, Time and Incarnation*, Oxford: Oxford University Press, 1969, p. 25.

74. _____, *Theology in Reconciliation*, Grand Rapids: Eerdmans, 1975, p. 12.

75. _____, *Space, Time and Resurrection*, Grand Rapids: Eerdmans, 1976, p. 186.

76. _____, *Transformation and Convergence in the Frame of Knowledge*, Grand Rapids: Eerdmans, 1984, p. 261. Cf. Walter Böhm, *Johannes Philoponos*, München, Verlag Ferdinand Schöningh, 1967, pp. 32-62, where light theory and the Episcopate of Alexandria are traced as the source of the thought of Philoponos. His was an effort to integrate consistently both the form and matter of the cosmos with the Creator, from which theological terms could be understood appropriately.

77. _____, *Reality and Scientific Theology*, Edinburgh: Scottish Academic Press, 1985, p. 5.

78. _____, *The Ground and Grammar of Theology*, Charlottesville: University Press of Virginia, 1980, p. 61.

79. _____, *Divine and Contingent Order,* Oxford: Oxford University Press, 1981, chapter two. See footnote 13. My interest in the concept of contingency began with this book. For an explication of the source and development of this doctrine in the Church see G. Florovsky, "The Concept of Creation in Saint Athanasius," SP, vol. VI, IV (1962), pp. 36-57, where the contingent nature of the creation developed by Athanasius is repeated by Cyril of Alexandria. This point is also the argument of Stanley Jaki's little book, *Cosmos and Creator*, Regenery Gateway, Inc., Chicago,

Gateway Edition, 1980. On p. 128 he writes: "The dichotomy will surprise no one moderately aware of the extent to which Christian thinkers can fall prey to the prevailing fashions of thought and the extent to which they are prone to fall back at all times on that most pagan of all ways of thinking, which prompts one consciously or subconsciously to eliminate the vista of contingency."

80. _____, *Christian Theology and Scientific Culture*, Belfast: Christian Journals, Ltd., 1980, pp. 86-87.

81. _____, "John Philoponos of Alexandria, Sixth Century Christian Physicist," <u>Texts and Studies</u>, vol. II, London, 1983, pp. 261-65.

82. M. G. Fouyas, *The Person of Jesus Christ in the Decisions of the Ecumenical Councils*, Ethiopia: Central Printing Press, 1976, p. 70.

83. Ibid., p. 70, footnote 25. Though Lebon, in his great study on Monophysites, does not mention Philoponos, he does contend that Severus argued for nothing more or less than the Christology of Cyril of Alexandria, a thesis which supports the call of Archbishop Fouyas. Cf. J. Lebon, op. cit., p. xxi.

84. Harnack, op. cit., vol. IV and V, p. 240.

85. P. Joannou, "Le premier essai chretien d'une philosophie systematique, Jean Philopon," <u>SP</u>, 5, 1962, p. 508.

86. R. Sorabji, *Time, Creation and the Continuum*, New York: Cornell University Press, 1983, p. 202. We live in a time when infinities and the human imagination require a disciplined role in knowing and being.

87. O. Culmann, *The Christology of the New Testament*, tr. S. C. Guthrie and C. A. M. Hall, Philadelphia: Westminster Press, 1959, p. 4, "... the discussion of 'natures' is nonetheless ultimately a Greek, not a Jewish or biblical, problem." Cf. Cyril Mango, *Byzantium*, New York, Scribner's, 1980, pp. 88-104. Although he perceives the debate politically of great consequence, he credits no sanity to the quibbling about the prepositions "of" and "in." See Karl Barth, *Church Dogmatics*, vol. I.1, pp. 375-79 for a corrective to this perception.

88. T. F. Torrance, ed., *Theological Dialogue Between Orthodox and Reformed Churches*, Edinburgh: Scottish Academic Press, 1985, p. 84. Indeed, it is fair to say that the apostate church is always the compelling force driving the True Church to create its "definitions" of the faith in Christ.

89. W. H. C. Frend, *Saints and Sinners in the Early Church*, Wilmington, Delaware: Michael Glazier, 1985, pp. 13-15. The Anathema of the Church should be traced back through Judaism to boundaries drawn by the ancient Hebrews, where the <u>holy</u> and the <u>profane</u> are important to the development of their view of the world.

Caesar I was, and am Justinian,
 Who, by the will of primal Love I feel,
 Took from the laws the useless and redundant;
And ere unto the work I was attent,
 One nature to exist in Christ, not more,
 Believed, and with such faith was I contented.
But blessed Agapetus, he who was
 The supreme pastor to the faith sincere
 Pointed me on the way by words of his.
Him I believed, and what was his assertion
 I now see clearly, even as thou seest
 Each contradiction to be false and true.
As soon as with the Church I moved my feet,
 God in his grace it pleased with this high task
 To inspire me, and I gave me wholly to it,
And to my Belisarius I commended
 The arms, to which was heaven's right hand so
 joined
 It was a signal that I should repose.

-- Dante, *Paradise VI*
trans. H. W. Longfellow

CHAPTER TWO

THE EMPIRE OF JUSTINIAN AND
THE COUNCILS OF THE CHURCH

In his excellent little book on *The Early Church*, Henry Chadwick has written, "The possibility of reconciliation with Monophysites haunted the long reign of Justinian (AD 527-565) and his wife Theodora."[1] The complexity of the forces influencing the shape which Justinian's Empire took is not readily apprehended by historians, and the Emperor has been viewed as everything from a demonical tyrant to the greatest and most creative of all the Caesars.[2] The dynamics operative in the spectrum of such a wide range of interpretation of Justinian's reign seem to defy evaluation. But that the age of Justinian was one of the great creative ages in the history of the world, and that the Imperial Rule intended to discover for Christendom a unity of the Church vital for the stability and strength of the legacy of Constantine and Livy to the history of the Roman Empire, cannot be denied. Both the plans for the reconquista at the borders of the Empire and for the renovatio in the Church were essential to the glory of Byzantium. The inner strength of the Empire could not be achieved by the mere streamlining of a culture's jurisprudence, but depended deeply upon the reality of its relation to God and His will for the nations. Military victory was, indeed, His favor upon the Empire's willingness to worship Him in spirit and in truth, and with Justinian we are compelled to realize that the Caesar of Rome and the Emperor of Byzantium had to be also a theologian among theologians. The royal decrees had to serve the authority of the unity of the Church of Jesus Christ if harmony and symphony throughout the Empire were to be achieved. The forces that would deny such symphony to the Empire were the very same forces that "haunt-

41

ed" its Emperor's struggles for a unified Church. It is within the context of these dynamic complexities that one must attempt to apprehend a life-setting for *The Arbiter* of John Philoponos.

The notice about Justinian in the <u>Paradiso</u> of the *Divine Comedy* by Dante implies that the Emperor's conversion to the two-nature formula of Pope Agapetus brought Justinian into relationship with the Church in such a manner that responsibility for the <u>reconquista</u> was completely delegated to General Belisarius, the Commander in Chief charged with the repossessing of the borders once established by Constantine. The Persian Empire, the Vandals of Africa, and the Goths in Italy all had to be defeated or controlled. To afford such campaigns required the communion of all five of the great Patriarchal Sees of the Church.[3] The necessary armies and sea power to establish the <u>Pax Romana</u> required huge sums of money and an imponderable fortitude. The same year, AD 533, that royal decrees affirmed to the Patriarchs of the Church throughout the Empire the four great councils of Nicea, Constantinople I, Ephesus, and Chalcedon, Belisarius had controlled the seas and was conquering the Arian strongholds in Africa. The forces of the great general of Justinian's reign affirmed to the Afro-Catholics the rightness of the royal condemnation of "The Three Chapters." By the time Justinian's Fifth Ecumenical Council could be ratified throughout the Empire, Italy and Spain had been restored to the <u>oikoumene</u>. Fortifications throughout the East saw Justinian's Christendom controlling the Caucasus that separated his reign from the Arabs and the Persian Empire, the Crimea, and the Danube against the Huns and Slavs. When he died in AD 565, Justinian ruled over a larger territory than any Emperor before him, and yet Frend records the exhaustive costs of this wearisome effort,[4] which we may find resonating with the Byzantine gazing at the failure of his Ecumenical Council to unite the East and

West of the Church.

Justinian's policy of reconquest required not only military might and money, but reliable fortifications and systems of transportation. The Emperor built cities, towns, churches, and roads with the same ardor that he provided ships and arms for Belisarius. As a result, the commerce and architecture of the Empire are without parallel in the Ancient World. Browning records that Procopius, the writer of *A Secret History* of Justinian's reign, "devoted a special work to a description, province by province, of the buildings constructed under his direction."[5] Both cities and churches, fortifications and houses of prayer, still stand today to teach us of the magnificence of his achievements. Not even turmoil and revolution in his capital could deter the tremendous energy with which his policies were executed. The Nika riot of 532, when Monophysites and Chalcedonians waged in the streets war between the Green and Blue parties of Constantinople and destroyed the Hagia Sophia, was not able to slow the <u>renovatio</u>. Helped by his wife Theodora, Justinian withstood the threats upon their lives at the hands of the mob, and rebuilt the perfection of the great domed church of Byzantium.[6] Critics have viewed both the longevity and beauty of the Hagia Sophia, not only as a climactic synthesis of the abstract and the plastic or pictorial which would point the race to the divine wisdom and light of the Pantocrator of the universe, but as "... one of the great turning points in the history of art."[7] Here was a point in time when, frozen in a perspective whose symphony with the divine turned human flesh to the eternal world beyond, the eye of the human soul could gaze upon the beauty of forever. The modern romantic poet of Ireland, W. B. Yeats, could write of it:[8]

> An aged man is but a paltry thing,
> A tattered coat upon a stick, unless
> Soul clap its hands and sing, and louder sing

For every tatter in its mortal dress,
Nor is there singing school but studying
Monuments of its own magnificence;
And therefore I have sailed the sea and come
To the holy city of Byzantium.

Besides the churches, monastic fortifications in support of city after city were established throughout the Empire. In the Wadi ed-Deir at the base of a shoulder of Mt. Sinai, the traditional site of the burning bush, Justinian dedicated St. Catherine's Monastery to the Theotokos. Forsyth writes of it:[9]

Certainly the determination and the administrative ability displayed in the construction of the monastery at Mt. Sinai bears witness to the disciplined vigor of Eastern Christendom under Justinian.

St. Catherine's stands until this day, the home of Orthodox monks, who guard yet the faith of Justinian and those treasures of their history which providence has allowed them to keep from the ravages of time, patrons, and conquerors.[10] Roads, bridges, and a vast trade and diplomatic service thrived in this administration. The silk worm was successfully brought from China in order to establish for the first time outside of the Orient a silk industry in Alexandria, an industry which has stood the test of time better than the city itself.[11] Horses and riders of the imperial cavalry were clad in mail for the first time in history, and both Goths and Vandals, Germans and Franks, found themselves contributing to a civil service which possessed extraordinary concerns for society. Perhaps because of Theodora's influence, women in particular and all those who wanted to leave un-Christian professions could find state refuge for new lives.[12]

Besides his supreme successes with military campaigns and the building of viable systems of building and commerce, Justinian is eminently remembered for his contribution to Roman law and jurisprudence. The Emperor conceived his administration of legal processes from Mesopotamia to

Spain to be profoundly related to the authority of the great Patriarchal Sees across the Empire, Old and New Rome, Jerusalem, Antioch, and Alexandria. The reconquista was intimately related with the renovatio of his reign, and his Institutes and Novellas were promulgated in Greek, in order to make his legislation readily available to Byzantium.[13] Of his penetration into the deep and intrinsic character of the relation between the State and the Church, perhaps it is best to allow him to speak for himself:[14]

> God's greatest gifts to men derive from his infinite goodness--the sacerdotium and the imperium, the first serving divine interest, the second human interests and watching over them: both come from the same principle and perfect human life. Hence nothing claims the Emperor's care so much as the honor of the priests, since they continually pray God for them. If the priesthood is sound and trusts completely in God and if the Emperor rules the polity entrusted to him with justice and honor, mutual harmony will arise which can only prove useful to the human race. God's true dogmas and the priest's honor are therefore our first care.

The royal majesty of the imperial throne must affirm and uphold the true substance of the faith of God. As a result, we can find the Bible admitted to the juridical process and guidelines for converted pagans among the law codes of Justinian.[15] The edict for the plan of the Code acknowledges the aid of Almighty God for this effort to clean up and clarify juridical law and extricate its abuse from a multitude of autonomies.[16] For the Emperor, no more could juridical law be free from the authority of the divine orders than the cosmos itself. Therefore, what Belisarius was to the military might of the Empire, Tribonian was to the legislative work, a lawyer whose expertise and energy provided a *Code of Law* for the world still influential today, and a *Digest* for law students which made practical for them a youthful grasp of civil service under the Almighty.[17] The so-called *Novels* of Justinian regulated with a sense of order and fairness the monetary policies in the Empire. Vasiliev quotes two of them:[18]

> ... to treat with fatherly consideration all the loyal citizens, to pro-
> tect the subjects against oppression, to refuse all
> bribes, to be just in sentences and administrative decisions, to
> persecute crime, protect the innocent, and punish the guilty
> according to law, and, on the whole, treat subjects as a father
> would treat his own children.

> ... it is imperative that the government taxes be paid in full
> and willingly at definite dates. Thus, if you will meet the
> rulers reasonably and help them collect for us the taxes with
> ease and dispatch, then we will laud the officials for their
> zeal and you for your wisdom; and beautiful and peaceful
> harmony will reign everywhere between rulers and ruled.

The *Codex*, *Institutes*, and *Digest* combine to form a formidable effort in jurisprudence. Ayer says of it that, "No body of law reduced to writing has been more influential in the history of the world."[19]

The harsh opinions of modern scholars on Justinian's throne should perhaps be tempered,[20] as one finds throughout the Orthodox Church of the East,[21] by an appreciation of the difficulty one seems to find whenever government under God would be expounded and practiced. For those who will not allow such exposition of life, no motive of Justinian could be intelligible enough to forgive him his failures, but for those who have ever ruled and desired justice done for the well being of those who are ruled, forgiving failure is as common as punishment for the guilty, and I think we do well when we are able to understand this difficulty and measure our leaders by their humanity under God and not their power and pride of place above us. Thus the great French scholar, Diehl, in his comprehensive study of Justinian's Empire, cautions us not to attempt to see the Emperor as all good or bad, but as capable with all of us of both. He sees Justinian taking seriously the inheritance of the Caesars from both Constantine and Augustus. Every aspect of his efforts, military, political, administrative, legislative, and diplomatic are only intelligible when they are entailed by his commitment to Christendom.[22] His failure to "christianize" the world and see in the external relations of a society the fruit of communion with the Pantocrator is not a failure easily criticized by us today. Surely without such temperance, we will never be able to penetrate into the motives and purposes of his religious policies, something absolutely essential for achieving an understanding of the life-setting of John Philoponos' *Arbiter*, and we shall find ourselves haunted by the very same forces which plagued Justinian's every effort to establish the dreams and goals of Byzantium, a truly Golden Age in the history the world.[23]

It is the judgment of modern scholarship that the backbone of the dream was the five great Patriarchal Sees of the Empire. Upon their unity and their dynamic relation with the throne of Justinian depended the stability and strength of the Empire. The Emperor need but seek that unity with the Church which would free the creative energies of Christendom to build in harmony and symphony with his reign the glory of God upon the earth. To seek such unity meant simply to reach that confession of Christ which would allow both Chalcedonians and Monophysites to agree to a common communion and fellowship, and Byzantium would shine and glow in the world.

The conflicts inherited by the Empire of Justinian can be traced back to the very beginnings of the Church's struggle against Ebionite and Gnostic thought developing in the early centuries. The fact that John Philoponos can refer to Paul of Samosata (AD 265-270) in his letter to Justinian is some indication of the role of memory in the confessions of the Church.[24] Paul of Samosata is for the Alexandrian Grammarian and for all the Orthodox a forerunner to the Nestorian development in the Dogma of Christ. We shall have to focus our attention now upon the significance of these assertions in the history of the Church and its creeds and councils. But we should keep in mind that the conflicts caused by the debates over Christ raged on all levels of society throughout Justinian's Empire. Henry Chadwick has pointed out that miracles could become tests of orthodoxy and that loyalty to party in the debate could lead to revolt in the streets of a city.[25]

Paul of Samosata is considered by most scholars to have expounded in his Christology a form of adoptionism.[26] His views, separating the Logos of God from the humanity of Jesus, are thought to provide the background for the perceptions of Arius of Alexandria. It was the passion of Athanasius against Arius which caused the Church of the fourth century its bitter disputes.[27] At Nicea (325) and Constantinople (381), it was the conceptual achievement of the homoousios of Athanasius which secured for the Church, against the adoptionism of thinkers like Paul and Arius, the ability to confess Christ as God. Admittedly, the homoousion was not a Scriptural term, but it was, Athanasius contended, a free invention of the Church's grounding in the Apostolic Ministry of the Holy Scriptures. It was very appropriate for the Church's confession in the face of the attacks upon it by those who could only see Jesus as one sort of creature or another and not as the Creator Himself.[28] The compellingness of the term's signification does not lie in any definition of the word outside of the usage of the Church, but in the context of the Church's expression of the Gospel received by the Fathers through the Apostles of Christ. Always, it was the salvation in Christ proclaimed by the Church which was the ground upon which the homoousion's appropriateness was justified, and it was the decision of the 250 to 318 bishops who met at Nicea that, within the boundaries set by Christ Himself, clothed with His Gospel, the Son of God was both one nature with the Being of God and one nature with humanity. The homoousion was necessary against the Arians to insure not simply a correct statement about Christ, but a truthful relation with the actual way God had chosen to reveal Himself and to accomplish reconciliation on behalf of mankind in the world. The necessity for the homoousion did not lie with the term itself, but in the way that it enabled the Church to point really to God and the salvation of His creatures in His Creation.

It was not until Constantinople I that the Nicene Creed reached its final form and the eternal and timeless begetting (γεννηθέντα) of the Son of God, the Creator, is affirmed by the use of his homoousion with the Father (ὁμοουσιον τῷ πατρί), and the Anathema upon people like Paul of Samosata and Arius of Alexandria was set in that concrete way which made them heretics to the Church throughout the history of the Councils.[29]

The fact that John Philoponos could, in his letter to Justinian, speak in the same breath of Paul of Samosata and Nestorius as under the condemnation of the Creeds is evidence that the homoousion did not once and for all time, however, settle the matter for the Church. Nestorius of Antioch, whom the Emperor Theodosius II (408-450) appointed Archbishop of Constantinople in 428, was evidently thrust into the subtleties of the dogmas and politics of the Church in the Empire at a depth that was beyond his capabilities.[30] Modern scholarship has tended towards seeing him as a hapless and inept victim of a rather ruthless champion of the Nicene-Constantinopolitan Creed, Cyril of Alexandria.[31] The debate is then analyzed as an antithesis between an Antiochan Christology, where a Sarx theology sought to stress the humanity of Christ, and the Logos theology of the See of Alexandria, where the divinity of Christ is emphasized.[32] The tension between the two perspectives provides the uncertain ground upon which ecclesiastical politics and the demand of an imperial pragmatism upon the structure of the Church create a history both complex and cruel in its disregard of the personal simplicity with which the believer is supposed to live. The impression is given that the substance of the faith is never finally the determining factor in the relations between Patriarchs such as Cyril and Nestorius. Granted that history has taught the Church no creed can in any ideal manner grasp the last word in the struggle to understand this substance, still it also teaches that the Church does really apprehend unto salvation her God in Christ, and it is the power of this reality, it is insisted, that must be found intelligible if she would evaluate properly the meaning of her history. How the one nature of the Eternal Son of God can be united with the one nature of Jesus, whose body was formed in the womb of Mary, so that Jesus Christ is at once both God and man, may be difficult to explain with any categories of thought the Church had yet been able to think, but the rational worship of the truth of God to which she was committed was formed in that way which no emperor could ever control.

Analyses of the debate between such men as Cyril and Nestorius in the Church, which would ignore the real struggle of this worship and mitigate its true influence upon the historical complexities accompanying that struggle, tend to understand its history in terms of moral and power politics of one sort or another. But the symbols formulated by the creeds were never intended as idealizations whose timelessness should suffice forever the believer in Christ. They were intended, rather, to point to that one who, quite beyond their statements of Him, was in fact the living God Himself, the God whose being and acts in the history of the race had been so impossibly preserved through the history of Israel and the Church in Holy Scriptures. Analysis of theologians like Cyril and Nestorius cannot be made in terms that reduce their concerns merely to political or moral categories. We are obligated, by the very character of their beliefs, to consider their debate primarily and most significantly as one in which what the reality of the salvation of the world by the love that God is in Himself was at stake.[33]

Thus, Chadwick has shown how the conflicts in the debate could effect the very heart of the priesthood of the sacraments, the Eucharist.[34] It was this Eucharist which, when championed in the fifth century by Severus of Antioch, the great Monophysite theologian exiled in Alexandria, led to the establishment of a separate communion from the imperially authorized communion of the Church in the Empire of Justinian.[35] Without a true resolution of these Christological problems, one in which the real substance of the faith could be explicated to the agreement of all the Sees of the Empire, the Imperium and the Sacerdotium could never form that symphony of purpose whereby the goodness of the Pantocrator might be administered to all. In this view, it is readily appreciated that no Emperor and no Patriarch of any See was ever able successfully to impose his private interpretation upon the Dogma of the Church.[36] The real power of revelation over the way theology should be done and over its relationship to political and ethical practices in society could not be denied. Upon it, the very unity of the Church and the strength of the Empire was seen to rely. Christendom for Justinian was a skin into which had to be poured the new wine of God, and a new world was required if he was to bring to the borders of Byzantium the Kingdom of God.

This meant that the resolution of the natures of Christ into a rational statement, over which the worship of the Church could agree to commune throughout the Empire, must be possible for human thought under the Pantocrator to achieve. It was upon this belief that Justinian sought to create a theology by which the Cyril of the Chalcedonian Creed and the Cyril of the Monophysites might be reconciled. It was this hope that led him to summon the Fifth Ecumenical Council of the One Holy Catholic Church of God in Christ. John Meyendorff has described this hope and belief as an effort which achieved "real progress in Christology."[37] To understand, we will have to see through the apparent failure of Justinian's achievement and into the true substance of the faith of Christ, and the real Sitz im Leben of *The Arbiter* by John Philoponos. To do this, a closer look at the issues between Cyril and Nestorius is necessary.

In the seventh chapter of *The Arbiter* by John Philoponos, where the Alexandrian scientist is attempting to think together the implications of the homoousion championed by Athanasius of Nicea and the hypostatic union in-sisted upon by those adhering to the theology of Cyril at Chalcedon, there is asserted the traditional argument against the arianism of Nestorius.[38] Philoponos understands that Nestorius did not find intelligible the hypostatic union in the Christology of Cyril (hd kynᵓ d-mltᵓ ᵓlhᵓ d-mbsr; section 23, line 15), which he claims is the confession faithful to the Fathers of Nicea (23.1-14). To understand this assertion properly, the Church developed together the concepts of the anhypostasis and the enhypostasis of the humanity of Christ by which is apprehended a union of the flesh with the Word that is ac-cording to nature and not simply a relation of will (23.17-25.4). Nestorian-ism could not understand the dynamics of these assertions and argued instead that the relation between the divine and human natures should be conceived to be one of divine illumination (mnhrnotᵓ ᵓlytᵓ; 25.8) or of divine dispensa-tion (mᶜbknotᵓ ᵓlhytᵓ; 25.12-13), where only an external relation to the man is posited. This relation is of love (ḥobᵓ; 25.17)[39] and not of nature, and does not allow Christ to be a man the way, say, Peter and Paul are men (25.19-24). Because of this, Nestorianism fails to grasp the significance of the con-cept of the anhypostatic reality of Christ's nature (ἐνυπόστατου εἶναί θαμεν την φύσιν ἐκείνην, lᵓ qnomᵓ l-kynᵓ ho ᵓmrynn; 26.1). Philoponos argues against the Nestorians that the enhypostatic reality of Christ's nature (27.1-6) must be understood in God in such a way that we do not conceive a humanity of

Christ which existed outside of the Word's actual assumption of flesh. To-gether these concepts affirm the reality of the individual man that Christ is, like Peter and Paul, as well as the natural union of that man with the Word of God, who is homoousion with the Father and the Holy Spirit. It is thinking ac-cording to the nature of the truth of a given reality that the Alexandrian sci-entist employs against the contentions of Nestorianism. The dynamics of the thought not only found enemies among those who would defend Chalcedon in a Nestorian manner, but also, as we have already seen, among the Monophys-ites who objected to the way the scientist conceived the relations between being or essence, nature, hypostasis, and person as they were compelled upon him by the realities of both the concerns of the Councils of the Church and the scientific culture of his Alexandria.

Modern scholarship has a tendency to question Cyril's real interest in orthodox theology and to question his political and ecclesiastical charac-ter.[40] He is often associated with the murder of the innocent Neoplatonist philosopher Hypatia.[41] And even though some compromise can be understood in his struggle against Nestorius when he does not attempt to impose his *Twelve Anathemas* upon the Council of Ephesus (AD 431),[42] still the tenden-cy is to dislike his character (Cyril never believed well of anybody!),[43] and even to consider his Christology, in virtue of his relation with Apollinarius, to be Monophysitic.[44] But I believe that Philoponos has rightly understood the debate between Nestorius and Cyril.

If we look even casually at *The Bazaar of Heracleides*, which was written by Nestorius in exile at Ephesus after a vicious struggle for author-ity with Cyril, it is readily seen that Nestorius, even to the end of his life, could not find intelligible Cyril's hypostatic union.[45] Driver, I think insight-fully, suggests that the real problem between the two Patriarchs must be found in the way that they attempted to think together the incarnation and the creation.[46] He lists in favor of Nestorius those things that Nestorius repeatedly denied in the work. Certainly, Nestorius does not ever intend to confess "two sons," of which he is commonly accused.[47] He certainly wants to confess the one person of Jesus Christ. But it is clear that he denies the unity of Christ is a "natural composition," however that composition might be conceived.[48] Nestorius began his thinking with the affirmation of the impassibility of the ousia of God.[49] The Word of God simply was not itself capable of becoming a man, since a man was a temporal being and the ousia of God was eternal and immutable. Nestorius worked out the relation in such a manner that the conjunction (ʿqypôtʾ ; 142.5) between them was in love (b-ḥôḇʾ) and not in ousia (b-ôsyʾ). It was in nature (b-kynʾ; 143.2) as one person, one equality, one honor, one authority, and one lordship. The person may be of nature (d-kynʾ) but he is not a nature. The person may be in nature, but he may not be considered a nature (143.2-8). For Nestorius, the nature and the ousia of the Father and Son may be one, but not as persons, so that he can believe he is in agreement with Athanasius and Nicea, while continuing to deny the identity of the person with the nature and the ousia of God.[50] Such an identity in his mind destroyed completely the humanity of Christ.[51] Because God the Word could not become the nature of a man, but only was in the nature of a man, the hypostatic union of Cyril was not possibly real (139.20-140.20; ḥdyôtʾ qnômytʾ).

The technical aspects of this argument were not for everyone. Those not trained in the science of the day could think that Patriarchs had too much time on their hands. But the confrontation did not take place on this level only. The difference between a relationship of love and a hypostatic union of the nature of God come as man could be explicated on a popular level with the confession of the <u>Theotokos</u>. The various subtleties about "in" or "of" nature and its identity might be lost upon the believers in the streets, but the cry of θεότοκος never went unheard by them. Mary could be for Nestorius the mother of Christ, but for him it was unscriptural to think she was the mother of God.[52] Wilken believes that the confession could not be made by Nestorius because he thought it meant that the Son was not truly God, and Cyril defended it because it guaranteed the Son was truly man, a paradox for the way the technical argument was being made,[53] but the crowds easily perceived that Nestorius' failure to admit that the Virgin was <u>Theotokos</u> meant that the son of Mary was not God, and Cyril in Alexandria never had much trouble enlisting popular support for his hypostatic union.[54] Cyril would see Nestorius condemned and sent into an exile which, however much sympathy we may give him today, marked his views throughout the development of the Dogma of the Church. By the time Philoponos wrote his chapter on the nature of the union in <u>The Arbiter</u>, it was common amongst all believers in the Church to repeat the Anathema of Nestorius and his teachings and followers. No matter how difficult are the paradoxes and the intricacies of the debate between Cyril and Nestorius, I believe we must learn to appreciate them if we are going to grasp the significance of the history of the Church's dogma. Frend thinks that Chalcedon partly vindicated Nestorius[55] and Patrick Gray has written a relentless argument showing that it was always the theology of Cyril that was being defended by the Councils and that was passed on to the age of Justinian.[56] Whether we are laymen or professionals today, whether Mary was the mother of God or not, and whether her son was God by nature or not, are issues that have as boundaries still the very salvation which began the tradition of the Anathema in the first place, a difference between the holy and the profane which must be discerned in a world that Christ with the

Spirit of His Father has created.

Perhaps it is too simplistic to attempt to understand the debate between Cyril and Nestorius as one that sees the Logos theology of Alexandria placed over against the Sarx theology of Antioch. Certainly, it was not the perception of John Philoponos that the debate could be analyzed in such a manner. In his time, evidently the difference between a relation of love and one of nature was vivid, and both Nicea and Chalcedon were understood in the sixth century to bear the assertion that the one incarnate nature of God the Word was homoousion with the Father and the Holy Spirit as well as with our humanity, the possessor of a mind and soul and body in a wholeness which compelled the Church to think together as best she could the doctrine of creation and the doctrine of incarnation. The difficulties we have with such thought, since the Anathema is involved, should not be shrugged off or put aside, for it has been indeed the history of the Church that she has been compelled to consider their significant influence upon one another with her confession of God.[57]

Because of the profound character of this debate, the Church has never really found the solution to the controversies. After Cyril died, his successors were not as compromising about his *Twelve Anathemas*. The debate continued to heat up and, in the midst of the struggles, Pope Leo of Rome was asked to provide a via media between the confession of Cyril and the claims of Nestorians, a clarification of the issues which would obviate for all, both West and East, the correct way that the Church should think of Christ. Chalcedon was the Council at which the Tome of Leo and the Twelve Chapters of Cyril were supposedly harmonized. The extreme positions of Antioch and Alexandria were to be avoided, both Nestorius and Eutychus were Anathema, both Arian and Gnostic traditions lay outside the boundaries which marked off the salvation the Church enjoyed. People tried to claim that *The Tome* said what Cyril said and *The Twelve Anathemas* said what Pope Leo said, but history has proven that the depths of the problems involved in thinking together the creation and the incarnation did not allow an easy penetration by human consciousness, and the controversies raged on into the reign of Justinian.

The conflicts thus involved the heart of revelation in the Church, the reality of reconciliation through the mediation of the person of Jesus Christ, the Creator of the cosmos and the Redeemer of the All, and challenged the believer with the profound personal objectivity of God with the world in such a way that all that we could understand was affected, as we have seen, even the most cherished of the Church's sacraments, the very heart of the priesthood, the Eucharist.[58] The difficulty of penetrating to a resolution of the Dogma in such a way that both East and West could agree that this was the rational worship in spirit and truth delivered once and for all to the Church is therefore understandable. But any actual resolution was not forthcoming. However popular the Theotokos and the communion were in the public eye, the reality to which the Church must point easily escaped the grasp of her attention.

We have already indicated the importance of confessing the Virgin as the God-bearer (yldt ʾlhʾ).[59] The union must be conceived to be between the Word and the flesh in Mary's womb (qnômʾyt ʾthyd l-bsr), in such a way that there is no time when the flesh existed outside the Word; i.e. other than simultaneously (hô kd hô ʾlhʾ b-hd w-brnšʾ). After this kind of union, it must be impossible to distinguish two hypostases (qnômʾ) which mingle (hlt) in a conjunction (b-nqypôtʾ) in any manner whatsoever, whether by authority (šôltnʾ) or command (pqôdôtʾ) or power (hyltnôtʾ). The union must be regarded as a natural union (hdyôtʾ kynytʾ). In no way must we be able to conceive of two Sons of God. Apart from the Eternal Word, there never was a time when the humanity of Christ existed. We may not speak of Christ as a God-bearing man (brnš⁾ hô šqyl 1-⁾1h⁾), but rather must we learn to speak of Him as the God He is in truth (⁾1h⁾ ⁾ytôhy b-šrr⁾), a nature (kyn⁾) of "the Word become flesh" (Jn. 1:14 --καὶ ὁ λόγος σάρξ ἐγένετο is translated into Syriac as d-hw⁾ m1t⁾ bsr⁾, an emphatic identification of the subject and the object with one another). The simultaneity of the uniting of the elements in the union is so stressed that the God-Man may not be conceived as a work simply to glorify God. He is by nature God Himself in His own glory (cf. the homoousios of Nicea). We worship only this one, the same, and not another, the same who is the Word become flesh and ascended to glory. This may not be conceived as some strange power which makes use of a spirit, but as His own One Spirit (dy1h hô roh⁾ yhyd⁾yt, cf. the homoousion of the Spirit at Nicea-Constantinople). The same is our High Priest and Apostle and Sweet-smelling Offering to the Father, the sinless God-Man of the Word become flesh. He alone gives life to mankind and only He saves mankind from its sin. He is, indeed, the first begotten from the dead.[60]

These assertions appeared to Nestorius to consume the humanity of Christ and destroy its reality. Against them, he struggled to protect a sense in which the full significance of the flesh as a man existed. Because he attributed to God's nature the properties of incorporeality (1⁾ mgšm⁾), infiniteness (1⁾ mstykn⁾), impassibility (1⁾ ḥšôš⁾ sk), and immutability (1⁾ mšthlpn⁾), he submitted that there is no cause whatsoever by which the Word can change. Therefore, there must be a conjunction (nqypôt⁾) which makes the Man equal (šw⁾) to the Word. The Word does not suffer except conjoined (nqyp) in a union with suffering man. Repeatedly, Nestorius speaks of one honor, one authority, one lordship (ḥd mš1ṭôt⁾, šwyôt⁾, ⁾ysr⁾) which exist of the Word and the Man.[61] He conceived the union of the divine and the human to be "in na-

58

ture" (b-kyn³). He uses this phrase over and over again throughout his argument.[62] The union in nature was not and could not be the <u>hypostatic union</u>
of Cyril's *Twelve Chapters*.

Because of this, Nestorius distinguishes between person (prṣôp³) and
nature (kyn³), so that nature signifies always what is universal and generic
while person must mean what is individual and particular. These categories
were commonly employed as the ABC's of the "Porphyrian Tree," the Neoplatonic analysis by which attempts were made to harmonize Platonic and
Aristotelian thought. The "Tree" was the methodological device which aided
the scientific student in an analysis of the realities of the cosmos and allowed
one to differentiate one thing from another thing.[63] The categories of genus
and species, the class-exclusion manner of definition of things, belong to the
development of this "Tree". In this manner, Nestorius could think that the
God-Man was one person but not one nature. The Trinity of God possessed a
nature, but not Christ. The Person of Christ was "in nature" equal in honor
and power and authority to the Son, who is one nature with the Father, but
the Son cannot be the same as the person Christ is in his nature (l³ hw³ gyr
hô m³ d-³ytôhy prṣôp³ b-kyn³ br³).[64] So because of the immutability of the
divine nature the <u>hypostatic union</u> of Cyril's thought was finally logically impossible to Nestorius.[65]

Summoned together in 451 AD by the Emperor Marcian, the Holy Fathers of the Church of Jesus Christ decided defnitively against Nestorius.
The Fourth Ecumenical Council of the One Catholic Church of God proclaimed
that the Cyrillian theology must be accepted. However, it was not oblivious
to the concerns of Nestorius over the real humanity of Christ. The Tome of
Pope Leo and the famous four adjectives of Chalcedon witness this aware-
ness. The natures united in the person of Christ were truly united. They were

59

without confusion or conversion (ἀσυγχύτως, ἀτρέπτως), so the Church could guard against every form of Docetic or Gnostic thought, and without division or separation (ἀδιαρέτως, ἀχωρίτως), so the Church could guard against every form of Ebionite or Arian thought. For the fifth century, this meant that both Eutychianism and Nestorianism were under the Anathema. The Tome, with its struggle at the Council of Ephesus and its concept of the <u>communicatio idiomatum</u>, was to be interpreted in such a way that all these kinds heresies were to be avoided.[66] The *Twelve Chapters* were fully accepted and the intelligibility of the hypostatic union of Cyril was to be fully realized. The two natures of the person of Jesus Christ were manifest in the one reality of Jesus even though they remained in <u>theory</u> distinguishable.[67] Christ was <u>in</u> two natures in such a way that he was one real person, the Son of God, in such a way that is, that Cyril and Pope Leo should be found to be saying the very same thing. It was a good compromise and a reasonable resolution of a very difficult subject. But history has proven such compromise to be inadequate in so far as it has been unable to compel the unity of the reasonable worship of the whole of the Church. The question could still be raised of the relation between the <u>one incarnate nature</u> of Cyril's Christology and the <u>one person</u> of the Tome. What did it mean to say 'in two natures' is that One who is Christ, rather than 'of two natures', as Chalcedon had finally done? The question could be raised and it was raised, with an intensity which was the inheritance that haunted the Empire of the great Justinian.

For most people, the debates between advocates of 'in two natures' and 'of two natures' as proper to the relation of the divine and the human in the union which was the person of Christ were probably held in arenas comparable to those where angels could be found dancing upon the head of a pin. Generally, as Chalcedon demanded, one could simply accept both of the formulas and acknowledge that Pope Leo's letter and Cyril's twelve anathemas meant to point to the same reality. But history demonstrates that mere convention, even when it means to be as tolerant and as well-intentioned as possible, is not the stuff of that kind of rational worship which must belong to the Church of God. The controversies that raged throughout the Roman Empire in the midst of the creation of Byzantine Civilization bear witness to a need that refuses to be resolved by mere convention. Penetration of our thought to apprehend the profound and compelling truth of God in Christ was demanded for such worship, and the struggle to accomplish this had to be pursued relentlessly by the Church.

Patrick Gray's monograph argues that the <u>Tome</u> was conceived only as an extension of Cyril.[68] He contends that the 'in' ($\dot{\epsilon}\nu$) of Pope Leo is meant simply to protect the Church from the notions of Eutyches, and resonates with the two adjectives that claim the natures are without confusion and division. The unity that was 'in two natures' could not be understood after the manner of Nestorius who grasped a difference between <u>in</u> nature and nature, and thus Cyril, though he preferred 'of two natures,' had accepted the phrase. The one incarnate nature of God the Word could be understood as 'in two natures,' but the two were distinct in that they were not known <u>in concreto</u> but with spiritual knowledge.[69] It was this spiritual knowledge that meant no emperor was ever free to impose upon the Church his private solution to the debates, and it was this spiritual knowledge, knowledge not of the ways that the race sought to worship God but of the way that God sought to reveal Himself to mankind, that was necessary for salvation. The Fifth Ecumenical Council commanded by Justinian a century after Chalcedon bears witness to the passions and the urgencies with which the East and the West of the Church would struggle to express the real significance of Cyril's hypostatic union for rational worship.[70]

The hundred years between Chalcedon and Constantinople II have often been neglected by scholars. The explication of the difference between 'in two natures' and 'of two natures' taxed the ability of priests and kings alike. The significance between the prepositions could not be penetrated without distinctions for which the world provided no ready examples. The necessity for disciplined thinking in such matters could be matched only by the rigors of the endeavors of a science in youch with the transcendent relations of real spiritual knowledge. It was not stuff for the popular imagination. No bishop should bother his flock with the sophistication that was required for such problems. Yet battles were fought on the streets of cities, in the churches, among monks in isolated towns, and in the royal courts of the Empire. Whole cities could even revolt against an Emperor because of the significance of the prepositions. The incessant squabbling and the violent emotions in the political realities in the debates does not make for easy reading. It is easy to want to ignore the history of the period. But I think Gray's effort to overcome the neglect is well placed.[71] The issues here, however exquisite they are for the realms of logic, remain fundamental to the witness of the Church in the world to Jesus Christ, and are therefore profoundly involved with the proclamation of the Gospel to the nations.

Gray's evaluation of Cyril's influence in the Councils is certainly not without its critics. Frend's interpretation of Cyril's hypostatic union continues even today the belief that his "one incarnate nature" smacks of a docetic tendency. He writes concerning the ἔνωσις καθ' ὑπόστασιν.[72]

> Yet for all this, Cyril's Christ remains an abstraction, his humanity so much part of the divine world as to be unrecognisable in human terms, and the salvation offered to man only intelligible in a pantheistic setting in which the destiny of the soul was reabsorption into the source of life whence it had come.

The West still finds Cyril's confession that the Theotokos gave birth to one of the Trinity the deification of man in such a way that Christ is not truly human. The East is still adamant about "the Master Theologian" of their traditions, and that those who followed him, among whom must stand the great Severus of Antioch, were not heretical Monophysites but "discriminators" who sought to guard against any Nestorian interpretation of the Tome.[73] Not surprisingly then, the history of the years leading up to the reign of Justinian is filled with the effects of debate. The ambiguities in the well meaning intention of Chalcedon could not be and were not ignored. Whatever the battle between the prepositions really meant, the Empire of Justinian was not at liberty to disregard its significance. There had been too much conflict over them throughout the Empires of his predecessors in the East and the West.

Both Gray and Frend recognize that Zeno's (AD 464-491) Henotikon represents the ultimate impotency of the Emperor to intervene in the profound and compelling source of ecclesiastical affairs.[74] In the East, especially in Alexandria, the Tome of Leo was "Jewish," and when Marcian had attempted to impose Chalcedon upon the Episcopate of St. Mark's See there was revolt in the streets of the city. Two thousand troops from Constantinople were required to quell the riots. Zeno hoped to overcome such tensions with his instrument of unity. The Henotikon proved successful throughout the East because it affirmed Nicea-Constantinople I, the Theotokos, and the Anathemas of Cyril, denying any docetism in his thought, and it claimed that Chalcedon intended the same. But it made no reference to the Tome of Leo, to which Rome had become absolutely committed, and there was nothing Zeno could do to reconcile the two parties in the debate. The reign of Anastasius (AD 491-518) saw the hardening of the chasm between Rome and Alexandria, and eventually the Eastern Empire, even though under Persian attack, would attempt to ignore Rome completely and unite itself around the Henotikon (Anastasius was assigned by Dante to the sixth circle of the Inferno, xi.8-9). It was under Anastasius that Severus, an ex-lawyer and a Syrian monk who became Patriarch of Antioch and the greatest theologian of the period, called the East to the 'royal road' of the spiritual knowledge, a way that would eventually lead him to establish a rival church to that of imperial policies. For with the reign of Justin I (AD 518-527), the support of the Emperor was shifted away from the Henotikon and Severus and the East found themselves under royal persecution. The Scythian monasteries had always remained in communion with Rome, and their domination of towns and cities, when Justin threw his support to them, proved more than able to rid Antioch and Palestine of Severus' ability to see to it that Leo's Tome which allowed one to conceive that Christ's acts were now one of a divine person and then one of a human person, was not accepted into the communion, so that the one being Christ could actually escape our attention.[75] The greatest theologian of Justin's Empire was soon made an exile in Alexandria and condemned by Justinian. He died in an Egyptian monastery on February 8, 538, his theology soundly rejected by the Empire's effort to support the reconciliation of the Sees. But the Monophysite Church had been firmly established by his relentless energy and labor and a separate communion permanently established in the Empire. The 'royal road' had not led Severus to the royal Church of the Empire, and the debate over the reality to which Chalcedon intended to point believers had defied every effort of Emperor after Emperor to discover that confession which would allow the rational worship of the Church to become unified throughout the Empire's Christendom. The sacerdotium and the imperium, regardless of how much one might have longed for their unity in the world, remained at odds with one another, to become a failed dream in history. Such unity proved to be for the Empire a skin into which we pour the wine of the natures of Christ with awesome trials and tribulations, no matter how important it is for the borders of the kingdom. It is this longing, however, that we must explicate if the life setting of *The Arbiter* is to be appreciated.

Justinian was actually an official in charge of religious affairs under Justin I, and had been deeply involved with Severus long before he ascended the throne in AD 527. He must have experienced early on in his career the difficulties caused by the Henoticon and the debate about the intention of Chalcedon between the East and the West. The fact that Severus did not embrace the Henoticon with much passion should be considered as evidence to his willingness to work out an appropriate confession by which the entire Empire might be united. As Frend writes, he "was a reluctant dissenter."[76] It is not until very late in his life, after at least two decades of open and honest discussions with Justinian and Theodora, that he was finally condemned and forced to establish a separate communion. Justinian is known to have been an Emperor who knew well the theological issues of his time. Justin I was probably relieved to give the government to him. If anyone could reconcile Severus and the East to Rome, certainly it must be the nephew of the theologically naive Justin. Mature and confident at the age of 45, Justinian sat down upon the throne and dreamed of an Empire that would at once be the restoration of the ancient glory of the Roman Empire and the triumph of the vision of Constantine, a Christendom to which the world must pay honor. From there he saw that Severus and his followers were indeed, unlike extreme Monophysites such as Julian of Halicarnassus, prone to reconciliation. Progress could be made towards unity among the five Patriarchal Sees if a compelling resolution to the debate could be achieved. If the ambiguities of Chalcedon could be clearly shown to point to the same realities of the Christology of Cyril, then a new and profound unity could be found beating in the heart of the Empire.

If we read any one of a number of the letters of Severus, we can easily realize that the great theologian was devoted to thinking together appropriately the homoousian of Nicea-Constantinople with the hypostatic union of Cyril made canonical at Chalcedon.[77] For instance, in the letter to Eupraxius, where Severus answers nine questions put to him about his teaching, we find a full explication of his teaching on Christ. The Son of God was eternally begotten of the Father as one nature (kyn²) and being (²ôsy²) with Him. The begetting must be conceived to be timeless, without beginning. Severus liked to use light as an analogy, always warning his reader that the created world provided helpful ways for our minds only to image what is finally an imageless or spiritual knowledge. The rays of the sun were one with the sun itself in such a way that you cannot think of the rays without thinking of the body which is their source. The Father and the Son were like that.[78] The Holy Spirit is never begotten but proceeds from the Father and must be distinguished from the Son. Both subsist, however, in individual hypostatic realities which are one nature and being with the Father. Therefore, we speak of the divine nature or being of the Godhead and of three hypostases or persons, each with its own individual characteristics or properties, of the One God. The One Triune God is the true God outside of which are the pretenses of Jewish monotheism and pagan polytheism.[79] Severus quotes from Cyril to justify finally this understanding of the Trinity.

He next considers the Incarnation.[80] The question is about how and in what way we are to conceive that the Word was incarnated. The Gospel of John and Paul's doctrine of Christ as the new Adam are behind the assertions of Severus. The removal of the ancient curse is bound up with the incarnation, death, and resurrection of the Word become flesh. It is in this light that we see ourselves out from under the curse of sin and in Christ. God, while remaining God, assumed by a true hypostatic union (b-ḥdyôt⁾ šryrt⁾ w-qnômyt⁾)[81] what we are. With the Theotokos, He took the seed of Abraham, so that the one Christ could give his life for us. The hypostatic union must be thought to have a divine beginning rooted in the eternality of the Godhead, and also a beginning in time with the God-bearing Virgin. God became what He was not while remaining that which He is.[82] To assure the ineffable glory of this knowledge, Severus denies Apollinaris his claim that the divine Logos replaced the human and fallen mind of the babe, and asserts the humanity of Christ is fully like our own with a rational and intelligent soul. The impassible nature of God in the hypostatic reality of the Word came as man among us in order to remove the curse upon us in Adam.[83] God is free to move outside of what He is in Himself with who He truly is into the world as a man without threatening the immutability of His being.

Next, Severus denies to Nestorius and his followers their assertions that the union is not of nature but an indwelling of the Word (w-ᶜmôdôt⁾ šḥymt⁾ yḥsḇyh l-mtbsrnôth d-mlt⁾).[84] The babe, the boy, the man from the Theotokos must be none other than the hypostatic reality of the Word,[85] wherein Paul says is the fullness of the Godhead. It is this One only who imparts to the Church the myriads of works of God, the gifts of the graces flowing severally throughout her members.

The question is then raised about such a nature that it can be at the same time divine in the Trinity and human in the Incarnation.[86] This is in fact the question that would lead the West to deny Cyril's "one incarnate nature" as proper to the Church's confession of Christ. Severus reveals much of his theological method here. The divine Scriptures with the Holy Spirit allow us to fix our minds appropriately upon the compelling character of divine realities. Thus committed to objectivities beyond our hearts, we understand that the Father and the Holy Spirit did not become incarnate, but only the Word, the eternal Son. We must never confuse the hypostatic realities of the persons of the Godhead. The Son, who is one nature with the Father and the Holy Spirit, became incarnate in his own hypostasis or person. For this, there is no analogy in creation, although we may, if we do not attempt to explain the invisible by appearances, use analogies as helpful to ourselves and always somewhat inappropriate to the divine objectivity. For instance, we may think of our speech as a clear image of our mind brought forth by our breath, and find a defective example, a shadow of the truth itself, to which the Scriptures would divinely point us. Thus, says Severus, we appreciate the use of the term nature. The statement that the Trinity is one nature and Christ is one incarnate nature means that we must allow the term nature to refer both to the being of God and at times to the hypostatic reality of Christ, just as we can employ it to refer to the common nature of mankind and to the individual nature of Peter. Nature refers in the one instance to a generic category, and in the second to an individual category, appropriately.[87] The incarnate nature of Christ refers to the individual hypostasis of the Word as a man. Language, claims Severus, is as good as its ability to refer us away from itself and to the given reality of an objective truth.

Severus goes on to employ once again the analogy of light. The objective truth to which the Church wishes to refer by her use of the term nature is spiritually discerned within the mystery of the revelation of God in Christ as divine light. This light shines and dispels the curse just as a light will dispel the darkness from a room. It shines unaffected by the dark just as the Word as man dispelled the curse from mankind's deafness. In Christ, the dust that was the destiny of the sons of Adam is made to be the sons of God as

68

light in God, free from the curse. It is in this light that Severus discusses the goats of Leviticus 16 and claims that, when people think of them typological-ly, they should not conceive them as two Christs, one passible and the other impassible.[88] The divine reality is that the impassible nature of the Godhead became in the hypostatic reality of the Word a man whose human nature has ineffably become one with the Word. This is the reality to which both Scrip-tures and the Holy Fathers intend to point the believer. Christ is One from two natures, both impassible and passible as eternity with time, perfect Godhead and humanity[89] (mn tryn kynyn ʾlḥôtʾ mšmlytʾ w-ʾnšôtʾ hd mšôdynn; from two natures, the complete divinity and humanity, we confess one [nature]). It is this One who is the offering for us, who suffered for us, and who gave us the victory over sin and death and the curse.[90] In this One is the wisdom and power of the eternity of God given to the second Adam, the God-Man, the Christ.[91]

As early as 1909, Joseph Lebon studied the works of Severus and concluded that his scientific theology was rooted in the Christology of Cyril.[92] In the hypostatic union, the relation of the human nature of Christ to the divine nature of the Son meant the evolution of the concept of "anhy-postasis."[93] The human nature of Christ only subsisted centered in the na-ture of the hypostatic reality of the Word, and never as an independent hypostasis. The two natures may be distinguished in <u>theoria</u> ($\theta\epsilon\omega\rho\iota\alpha$), but in reality they are one nature, one hypostasis, one person,[94] for it is not pos-sible for a person or hypostasis to exist except with a nature.[95] This was in line with Athanasius, Gregory of Nazianzus, and Cyril. The point is always that the one reality which is the person of Jesus Christ subsists in this world as an absolutely unique reality rooted in God the Word.[96] This compound na-ture of Christ ($\mu\iota\alpha$ $\phi\upsilon\sigma\iota\varsigma$ $\sigma\upsilon\nu\epsilon\tau\sigma\varsigma$) was employed by the doctors of the Church as fundamental to the given reality of the revelation, and no scientific theology could be developed without apprehending the "anhypostatic" existence of the human nature of Christ. Lebon notes, by the way, that it was this theology that John Philoponos attempted to explicate for the Fifth Ecumenical Council of the Church summoned by Justinian at Constantinople in AD 553.[97] With Chalcedon, two natures after the union may be accepted, and both Nestorianism and Eutychianism may be denied, but these natures are intelligible only in theory, being in reality one nature,[98] without possibility of dividing the person of Jesus Christ into two. In this appreciation of Severus, Lebon recognized the necessity of understanding the term nature in a "pleonastic" way, where the semantic range is determined in particular contexts by the reality to which the language intends to point the reader.[99] In this he quotes Junglas:[100]

> Dass bei Severus die Begriffe φύσις und ὑπόστασις identisch sind, zeigt zunächst ihr synonymer Gebrauch; öfters stehen sie pleonastisch nebeneinander.

What was important was not the definition of the term in and of itself, but the way it was used in particular contexts to point to the intelligibility of given realities. In thinking together its use in Trinitarian thought with its use in Christology, the scientific methodology of Severus demanded the term be understood appropriately in the light that the Word of God actually is for us. It was not fitting for "accurate doctrine"[101] that the term should refer in the same way to the Trinity as it referred to Christ. The nature that was homoousion with the Godhead in the hypostatic reality and person of the Word became the center of being for the human nature of Christ, and in this sense the μία φύσις τοῦ Θεοῦ Λόγου σεσαρκωμένη intends to point to the same reality as the two natures of the One Person of Chalcedon, since no Nestorianism or

70

Apollonarianism was ever intended there or at Nicea-Constantinople.[102] Leo's Tome and Cyril's Twelve must intend to point to the same unique reality which was the mystery of God in Christ revealed to the Church. Reconciliation in the debate between the West and the East must therefore be possible.[103]

At least, it appeared that way to Justinian. The newly enthroned Emperor sanctioned harsh measures against all those who would not attempt to apprehend afresh the problem of the "natures" identified with Jesus Christ, the Savior of the world. The Henoticon represented a failed effort because it attempted to bypass Chalcedon, and Chalcedon's adverbs were necessary against Docetic and Ebionite tendencies in the development of the Church's thought. However, Cyril must be understood as canonical and the hypostatic union of the natures proclaimed to be the intention of Chalcedon. There must be a via media able to apprehend the rational worship of the Church. Justinian thus laid down his policy concerning the confession of Christ in his reign. Anyone who would not desire the unity of the Church throughout the Empire, and therefore the strength and tranquility of the throne, could be considered an enemy of his government and liable for punishment.[104] Henry Chadwick well writes, "The possibility of reconciliation with the Monophysites haunted the long reign of Justinian (527-565) and his wife Theodora."[105]

Two aspects of this policy demanded resolution. Monophysite objections to Nestorian sympathizers at Chalcedon had to be met, which meant that Theodoret of Cyrus and Ibas of Edessa, disciples of Theodore of Mopsuestia, along with Origenistic tendencies to divorce the nature of the Father and the Word, had to be refuted. This effort has come to be known as the affair of the "Three Chapters." Given this appeasement of their concerns, Monophysites had to acknowledge the ecumenical authority of Chalcedon and embrace its confession as in agreement with the Deposit of Faith inherited from the divine Scriptures and the Holy Fathers at Nicea-Constantinople.

In an excellent article presented to a symposium on "Justinian and Eastern Christendom" at Dumbarton Oaks in 1967, John Meyendorff reviews the dynamics of religion in Justinian's reign.[106] It is in the midst of an incessant military struggle as well as a relentless need to build and restore the Roman Empire that we must attempt to understand the forces of the Christian oikoumene of Justinian's religious policy of imposing unity upon his subjects. To bring Rome, Constantinople or New Rome, and the Patriarchal Sees at Antioch, Jerusalem, and Alexandria into a unity that would effectively create a dynamic employment of the forces involved was an ambition that coincided with the Emperor's military and economic programs. He had to use everything from direct coercion to free theological discussion with the opposing parties. Ecclesiastical policy and imperial laws profoundly influenced one another,[107] and the reconquests of Spain, Africa, and Italy could affect that point in the spectrum between coercion and discussion at which the Emperor's policy might be administered. Meyendorff's quote of Justinian's own statement on the relation between the sacerdotium and the imperium is worth repeating:[108]

> There are two greatest gifts which God, in his love for man, has granted from on high: the priesthood and the imperial dignity. The first serves divine things, while the latter directs and administers human affairs; both, however, proceed from the same origin and adorn the life of mankind. Hence, nothing should be such a source of care to the emperors as the dignity of the priests, since it is for their (imperial) welfare that they constantly implore God. For if the priesthood is in every way free from blame and possesses access to God, and if the emperors administer equitably and judiciously the state entrusted to their care, general harmony (συμφωνία τίς ἀγαθή) will result and whatever is beneficial will be bestowed upon the human race.

It was a symphony that was difficult to direct, but none can doubt Justinian's intent to hear it played. The juridical law was thus employed to give imperial authority to sacred judgments; conciliar decisions were made laws by imperial edicts. The traditions of the five ancient Sees could compete for influence effecting the politics and economy of the Empire, and could deny the Emperor any decision with which he could make laws. It was not a symphony easily realized. Meyendorff claims it was a part of Justinian's greatness that he realized the limitation of his power in doctrinal matters of the Church, for it was this realization that caused him to become as sensitive as possible to the issues and to push for a real development of Christian thought.[109] Old Rome might assure the East that "one of the Trinity" died for the world and Monophysites who were not Julianists might find a resolution to the difference between the East and Pope Leo by saying that one was in two natures (ἐν δύο φύσειν) or of two natures (ἐκ δύο φύσεων), and real progress in thought could provide the ground upon which the symphony might be played. It was not enough merely to defeat the Goths in Italy. It was also necessary that Old Rome and Alexandria should be able to confess in concert the reality of the Savior of the world. To accomplish such progress, Justinian's policy led inevitably to a fifth Ecumenical Council for the Church. In AD 553, he summoned the Holy Fathers to Constantinople, hopeful they would be able to achieve that development. Beyond the ambiguities of the Tome and the docetic appearance of Cyril's hypostatic union must exist that rationality which would point all concerned to Christ, in whom was the salvation of the Empire and all mankind.

It will prove helpful, I believe, at this point to consider the forces that helped to shape the life and cause the early death of a contemporary of John Philoponos, called in his own way to set his mind to the task of contributing to the development for which Justinian longed, Anicius Manlius Severinus Boethius of Rome, who was executed in a prison at Paris a year or so before Justinian's enthronement. Henry Chadwick records how Beothius, in Rome in order to enlist the support of Pope Hormisdas for Justinian's budding plans, overheard Scythian monks arguing for the acceptance of the Theopaschite formula.[110] They believed it was the key to a <u>via media</u> between the East and the West. Boethius was disconcerted by the lack of disciplined thinking among the Bishops and the Roman Senators. Evidently, he was no sceptic who believed that, because of the confusion caused by the linguistic fog surrounding the debates over the prepositions and the natures, there was no rational and logical solution to the problem (two-nature Christology cannot produce a unity of person and one-nature Christology must mean the loss of the humanity of Jesus). He set himself the task of writing his tractate "Against Eutyches and Nestorius."[111] He would attempt an explanation utilizing the training, in which he had excelled for the greater part of his influential life, in the scientific disciplines of his day. Chadwick attaches great significance to Boethius' effort:[112]

> Pope Hormisdas' Roman theologians came to think better of the Scythian monks and their theopaschite formula, and this shift is probably to be attributed to the influence of Boethius' fifth tractate.

Certainly, it was helpful to the policy being formulated in New Rome by Justinian. The Emperor had already seen the willingness of the followers of Severus to accept, however reluctantly, the "in two natures" of Chalcedon if "one of the Trinity died for us" was acceptable to the interpreters of the Tome. Boethius, for his part, was sure the Tome was only intended to guard the Church against Eutychianism and was not in any way intended to be in sympathy with Nestorianism. He believed it must be possible to lift the linguistic fog and see through the confusion surrounding the confessions. To this purpose, he set his mind for the task.

Boethius begins the tractate embracing the homoousion of Athanasius against Arius and the distinction of persons in the Trinity against Sabellius, understanding Nestorius to possess an Arian tendency and Eutyches a docetic one. He begs the overseeing of his spiritual father, John the Deacon, expresses his belief that the argument over the prepositions can be overcome, and begins his analysis by attempting to define the critical terms in the controversy. Chadwick lists four definitions of the term nature which were evidently a part of Boethius' academic training.[113] In the first place, nature according to the Neo-platonic tradition embodied in Ammonius, the teacher of John Philoponos in Alexandria, is "a term for those things which, insofar as they exist, can in some way be apprehended by the intellect."[114] This definition is bound up with concepts which separate the intelligible world from the sensible world and posits timeless rational forms as necessarily related to the divine as the source of the rationality of the human soul or mind. This tradition recognized value only in that which was eternal, where the problem of being and nothingness is resolved as nature is given to unformed matter, a kind of nothing, and evil is identified with "the defection from being towards nothingness." Secondly, nature is defined in Plato in terms of substance, physical or incorporeal. It is "that which can either act or be acted upon," where again eternal forms are the rational substance for the nature of an immortal soul. Aristotle provides the third definition of nature and restricts the term to refer to physical substances only, and each nature is accorded a proper movement by which the purpose of the cosmos is generated, where the accidental lies outside of the grasp of scientific knowledge.

And finally, also from Aristotle, is a definition of nature which "gives form to each thing." In this definition, nature is a term which can entail both formed and unformed substance and person or hypostasis entails

75

only an individually formed thing.

Chadwick claims Boethius does not make it clear which of the definitions he uses in the Christological context, but some things are evident. Boethius is quite clear that it is Pope Leo's statement in the *Tome* declaring that the natures in Christ do, in communion with one another, what is proper to each, which is the source of the debate. The Word's nature does what is appropriate to the Word and the human nature what is proper for humanity (agit enim utraque forma cum alterius communione quod proprium est) is a statement which can be interpreted in a Nestorian manner.[115] By utilizing Aristotle's definition of nature in its broadest sense and the Porphyian Tree of the Neo-platonic tradition, Boethius distinguishes nature from person in that nature refers to what is generic and person to what is a species. Chadwick points out that Boethius is very aware of the translation problems between Greek and Latin,[116] where "persona," for instance, can mean the mask of a character in a play and "prosopon" means a particular hypostasis and does not readily translate person. How this is worked out, observes Chadwick, depends upon the manner in which Aristotelian categories are understood within Platonic universals, and he sees inconsistencies in Boethius' argument.[117] Yet it is clear that for the Roman Scholastic a sharp distinction must be made between nature and person by which person is ultimately identified as a species of man who is a rational, mortal animal. Nature in this case is the genus of animal over against inanimate things, mortal over against angels and gods, and rational over against the beasts. It is this definition, by the way, which comes down to us through Ratramnus, Peter Lombard, and Thomas Aquinas.[118] It was attacked in the twelfth century by Richard of St. Victor on the grounds that it could not refer to God since the Divine Persons could not be individualized in the manner in which Boethius had understood

person. That is, we cannot understand φύσις by reading back into it a definition of <u>natura</u>, and we cannot understand by reading <u>substantia</u> back into it,
and we cannot understand ὑπόστασις by reading <u>persona</u> back into it.[119] Chadwick sees that ultimately the fog was not lifted by Boethius at all. He
writes:[120]

> All that is certain is that the Father, Son, and Spirit are not words
> separately expressive of substance, and that in the Holy Trinity
> relation is eternal and not accidental.

What is certain, however, and important to understand if we are to
distinguish the scientific methodology of Boethius from that of John
Philoponos, is the fact that the Roman Scholastic understood the nature of the
human body as mortal and the nature of the soul as immortal. Boethius sees
an image of man which corresponds to the Aristotelian physics and the Platonic metaphysics common in the Ptolemaic Universe of his time. Whatever
unity he could explicate finally succumbed to the idea that God was ultimately
unknowable in Himself, except by revelation. Chadwick writes of him:[121]

> Boethius' juxtaposition of Neoplatonic logic and Christian theology
> rests on a two-source view of truth. Revelation and reason are seen
> as parallel ways of discerning reality ... he is ready to envisage
> the parallel affirmation of two truths which reason cannot
> reconcile.

Against the sceptics, Boethius must have felt defeated and the <u>via
media</u> must have seemed like only a dream, little enough consolation for a
man who would soon be executed for treason.[122] Advocating a mystical leap
of faith away from the compelling claims of rational worship upon the Church
was not the stuff of which Royal Decrees are made.[123] Justinian could not
possibly use the tract to further his policy of reconciliation. However much
persuasion the argument had in causing Roman Bishops to embrace the Scyth-

ian Monks, something more would be required for Patriarchal Sees and Church Councils. The <u>via media</u> must be explicated in that way which would compel rational agreement of committed and holy Fathers of the Church who required to assent with their minds to the truth of God's salvation in the world. Perhaps the Scythian Monks did encourage the Emperor's growing hope for unity, since Rome seemed ready to compromise with at least one of the demands of the East. Perhaps Boethius' effort was enough to cause Justinian to think the problem could be worked out if the right scientist would apply himself to it. Perhaps where ecclesiastical minds could not penetrate, a really trained scientist reasonably could. I like to think that thus Justinian's policy of free discussion was extended to the Alexandrian Scientist John Philoponos. On the hard road to Church unity, which Justinian was determined to take, I like to see the Emperor turning to appoint perhaps the greatest Christian physicist of the time, hoping to provide for the Bishops and the crowds across his Empire something a little more solid than what Boethius had provided the Monks and the Romans. It is in this context, a royal appointment to Arbiter in the controversy, that I believe Philoponos composed *The Arbiter*.

We should remember here that Justinian's relation with Severus of Antioch, often mediated by the Empress Theodora, deteriorated through the years leading up to the Fifth Ecumenical Council, and however much we come to understand the theology of Philoponos in relation to the great theologian of the East, we will have to allow that the Emperor did not see the Alexandrian scientist in the same way as he viewed Severus. Severus will prove to be unable to continue his dialogue with the Imperium, and, however much he desired to see a unified Church in the Empire, he will find himself committed at last to a separate communion. Justinian condemned him at this point with all the force available to him, and Severus, even while crowds flocked to his communion, found himself once and for all an exile. Indeed, in 537 he was compared to Nestorius and the anti-Christian philosopher Porphyry.[124] But at this time Philoponos was probably just beginning to be able to conceive of *The Arbiter*.[125]

Be that as it may, the important thing in our study is to notice that, in spite of the hardness of the road, Justinian continued to will to hear Bishops and Scientists alike in order to discover the via media for his Empire. He must have been hopeful that, with the acceptance of the Theopaschite Formula in Rome, the affair of the *Three Chapters* might finally set the stage for a new agreement between Old and New Rome and the East. It was clear to him that the way must lie along the lines that could be drawn by a Cyrillian interpretation of Chalcedon. The four adverbs and the two natures of the union were necessary and acceptable in the East, as protection against Nestorianism and Apollinarianism. The μία φύσις of Cyril and Athanasius guaranteed the unity of the one Son of God, the Word become flesh. The relation between nature and person was all that seemed to divide the parties. Surely some resolution of it would be forthcoming. If Christ is "in two natures" or "of two natures," he must also be in some sense one reality and surely all intended to point all the world to this one. Upon the Fifth Ecumenical Council and its ability to resolve this problem, at last, depended the fate of Justinian's dream. Gray has persuasively written:[126]

> He alone understood the Chalcedonian problem could be solved only if the solution was found in which acceptance of Synod and Tome was combined with a Cyrillian interpretation of Chalcedon.

Constantinople II bore the responsibility of proclaiming Jesus Christ in such a way that the five great Patriarchal Sees would be united and bring to the Empire a new stability and strength which would allow to prosper one of the greatest kingdoms the world had ever experienced. It is strange for us in our modern world to think that upon the Church's witness to Christ depended the glory of Byzantium, but it was common belief then and perhaps we would do well to try to understand it better. Certainly, there is no real understanding of Justinian without its appreciation. Diehl's great study of him acknowledges that, good or bad, he was the Emperor of the Ancient World, one whose achievement could look back at Solomon's glory without envy. No one contributed more to free discussion and debate over the possibilities of reconciling Christendom's splits in a hostile world, and every aspect of his efforts--political, military, administrative and legislative, economic, diplomatic, and religious--was dynamically concerned with this witness. He might be wise, he might be foolish, but he was a Caesar whose failures and grandeurs were thoroughly Christian,[127] and a thoroughly knowledgeable one at that. Here is his decree of AD 551, anticipating the Fifth Ecumenical Council:[128]

> In recognizing in both natures (that is, in divinity and in humanity) our One Lord Jesus Christ the Word of God made flesh and made man, we do not introduce into his own hypostasis a sharp division into parts, but rather we signify the difference of natures out of which he is composed, a difference which is not done away with by the union, since each nature exists in Him. For when the composition (σύνθεσις) is confessed, the parts subsist in the whole, and the whole is known in its parts. The divine nature is not changed into the human nature, nor is the human nature turned into the divine nature. Rather, since each of the natures that belong [to Christ] is understood in the limit and proportion of its own nature, we say ἕνωσις καθ᾽ ὑπόστασιν. This union by hypostasis shows that the divine Word (that is, the one hypostasis out of the three hypostases of divinity) was not united to a man who subsisted in an hypostasis before (προϋποστάντι ἀνθρώπῳ) but created for himself in the womb of the Virgin, in his own hypostasis, flesh animated by a rational and intellectual soul, such as human is. Accepting also Cyril's saying, "one incarnate nature of the Word of God," we confess that One Christ was completed out of the divine nature and the human nature; not one nature, although some people, misunderstanding the saying, attempt to say the latter. Of course the father, when he said, "one incarnate nature of the Word," intended thereby the word "nature" to have the sense of "hypostasis." In whichever book he uses this expression, he has for the most part made it clear in what follows,

where he says "Son" or "Word" or "only-begotten," that the reference is not to anything as nature, but rather as hypostasis or prosopon.

It was not a decree for new believers or the crowds on the streets of the cities, but it was certainly a royal, however strained, effort to achieve a resolution. Leo's Tome intended to point to One Christ, One Son. Cyril never intended to confuse or mix the natures. They both intended to witness to God's salvation in the Savior of the world.

John Meyendorff has asserted that the age of Justinian should be understood as one in which real progress was made in Christology.[129] He has written about AD 553, when Justinian's Decree would be tried by the Council:[130]

> It is at this point that his great dream of a universal empire, united politically and religiously, as well as his personal theological mind which understood well the issues dividing Chalcedonians and Monophysites, were put at the service of a religious policy which led to the Fifth Council at Constantinople (553).

The Decree and finally the Council had to face many problems. Old Rome doubted that New Rome could condemn the *Three Chapters* and still claim to honor Chalcedon. The disciples of Severus already knew very well one could not have a hypostatic reality which did not possess in some way its own nature. But in spite of these problems, the resolve of Justinian established for all concerned the necessity of realizing that words and language did not contain in themselves the realities which they intended to communicate. This realization, along with the scientific principle that truth was prior to our understanding or thinking about it, was a long way towards freeing the Church for discussion. I believe John Philoponos was quite at home with these developments and counted himself a subject of a wise and well-intended Emperor. His letter to Justinian, in which he defends the main thrust of the argument of *The Arbiter*, and declines an invitation to visit the Throne at

Constantinople because of his old age, is evidence that, unlike Severus, the Alexandrian Scientist continued to enjoy as a critic of Chalcedon a friendly relation with the Emperor.[131] Even in the midst of the creative synthesis Justinian was attempting, coercion was not the only means he employed to persuade those who continued to debate towards a reconciliation. Again Meyendorff writes:[132]

> This content of Christian theology of the Justinianic age deserves, especially in our times, greater appreciation than it is generally given... it is important to recognize that the great debates of Justinian's reign were theologically among the most fruitful of Christian history, and may prove to be of special and rather unexpected relevance in the light of our own modern categories of thought.

The via media, like the Hagia Sophia and the Monastery at Mt. Sinai, still stands today to remind us of Justinian's creative concerns for Christendom in the world. Their enigmatic character still persists in reminding us that the old and the new must be profoundly and deeply related in all true progress. *The Arbiter* of John Philoponos begins its argument with an exhortation to its reader that truth is capable of revealing itself to that eye whose soul sincerely searches for it.[133] It was the premise that would allow the scientist his investigation of an order whose uniqueness and profundity made Byzantium long for that marriage between the human and the divine over which all the ages of the world could rejoice. Divine intelligibility with the world's history seemed to call out to us for our attention. What that tradition was in the Academy of Alexandria, where John loved to labor in Christ, must be the subject of our next chapter. We will try to penetrate his world in such a way that we will be able to apprehend the significance of the scientific culture for the life-setting of *The Arbiter*.

NOTES TO CHAPTER TWO

1. H. Chadwick, *The Early Church*, op. cit., p. 208.

2. W. Frend, *The Rise of Christianity*, Philadelphia: Fortress Press, 1984, pp. 828-68.

3. J. M. Hussey, ed., *The Cambridge Medieval History*, Cambridge: Cambridge University Press, 1966, p. 21. "The accession of the orthodox Justin in 518 restored communion with the West, which was to prove essential for the reconquest of Africa and Italy by his nephew Justinian."

4. Frend, *The Rise of Christianity*, op. cit., pp. 854-56.

5. R. Browning, *The Byzantine Empire*, New York: Scribner, 1980, p. 37.

6. J. Beckwith, *Early Christian and Byzantine Art*, London: Penguin, 1970, pp. 44.

7. I. Hutter, *Early Christian and Byzantine Art*, New York: University Press, 1971, pp. 72-74.

8. W. B. Yeats, "Sailing to Byzantium" in *Modern American Poetry, Modern British Poetry,* ed., L. Untermeyer, New York: Harcourt, Brace, and Company, 1950, p. 117 of Modern British Poetry.

9. G. H. Forsyth, "The Monastery of St. Catherine at Mount Sinai: The Church and Fortress of Justinian," DOP 22 (1968), pp. 3-19.

10. E. E. Freeman, "The Rediscovery of Codex Syriacus," in Alumni/ ae News, Princeton Theological Seminary, vol. XXIV, no. 4 (Fall, 1985), pp. 3-6. It is reported here that modern technology's ability to read this palimpsest gives us the earliest manuscript witness to the Gospels.

11. J. M. Hussey, op. cit., p. 37.

12. W. H. C. Frend, *The Rise of the Monophysite Movement*, Cambridge: Cambridge University Press, 1922, p. 260, see footnote 1. The Empress' influence in the Empire extends well beyond social work, however, and is vital for understanding Justinian's policies towards Monophysites.

13. Frend, *The Rise of Christianity*, op. cit., p. 829.

14. Hussey, op. cit., p. 436, where a Roman Pope is cited as thanking the Lord for Justinian's imperial and priestly soul.

15. P. R. Coleman-Norton, *Roman State and Christian Church*, London: SPCK, 3 volumes, 1966. See vol. III, pp. 1048-49, 1053, 1125-27.

16. Ibid., pp. 999-1000, 1016.

17. A. A. Vasiliev, *The Byzantine Empire*, Madison: University of

Wisconsin Press, 1952, pp. 142-47. This is perhaps the most comprehensive account of Justinian's reign in English.

18. Ibid., pp. 159-60.

19. J. C. Ayer, *A Source Book for Ancient Church History*, New York: Scribner's, 1952, p. 541.

20. In the shift the author has evidently taken in his comments on Justinian, Frend has, I believe, shown us the way here.

21. A. Gerostergios, *Justinian the Great*, Belmont, Mass.: Institute for Byzantine and Modern Greek Studies, 1982.

22. C. Diehl, *Justinien et la Civilisation Byzantine au vi^e Siécle,* 2 vols., New York: Burt Franklin, 1901. See vol. II, pp. 661-62.

23. E. R. Hardy, "The Egyptian Policy of Justinian," DOP, 22 (1968), pp. 23-41. This article surveys admirably the king's struggle and suggests that, in the decade following the rebuilding of Hagia Sophia, it seemed possible to Justinian that he would indeed succeed with his dream.

24. A. Šanda, op. cit., p. 126.

25. H. Chadwick, "Moschus and Sophronius," in *History and Thought of the Early Church*, London: Variorum, 1982, pp. xviii, 1-74.

26. Eg. Frend, *Saints and Sinners*, op. cit., pp. 144- 45, 150-51.

27. F. Young, *From Nicaea to Chalcedon*, Philadelphia: Fortress Press, 1983, pp. 57-83.

28. P. Schaff and H. Wace, *Nicene and Post-Nicene Fathers*, Grand Rapids: Eerdmans, vol. IV, 1978 (1891), see "De Decretis," pp. 150-72. The problem generally involves the distinctive natures of the eternal begetting and the birth of the Son of God.

29. Schaff, *Creeds of Christendom*, vol. 2, Grand Rapids: Baker Book House, 1977, pp. 57-58. See also K. Barth, CD, vol. I.1, ed. G. W. Bromiley and T. F. Torrance, Edinburgh: T. & T. Clark, 1975, pp. 438-441.

30. Frend, *Saints and Sinners*, op. cit., p. 149.

31. Young, op. cit., p. 244.

32. T. F. Torrance, *Theology in Reconciliation*, Grand Rapids: Eerdmans, 1975, pp. 215-66. The author shows that the scientific methodology of Athanasius in Alexandria provided a theologia dependent upon the inherent and intrinsic nature of reality in such a way that the Logos-sarx and the Logos-anthropos distinctions are distorting categories upon which to base any analysis of the meaning of God in Christ.

33. Ibid., p. 248. "To know God kata physin, in accordance with his own nature, is to know him under the impact of his distinctively divine energeia, that is, to know him through a living empirical relation determined by theosis." Cf. K. Barth, CD, vol. I.1, op. cit., pp. 378-79 for a modern state-

ment on the force of the truth of God in the midst of socio-cultural and political powers.

34. H. Chadwick, "Eucharist and Christology in the Nestorian Controversy," in *History and Thought of the Early Church*, op. cit., pp. xvi, 145-64, where the intelligibility of ἕνωσις καθ' ὑπόστασιν is the basis for a eucharist that guarantees the resurrection of the body and the συνουσία with the Logos of God, an assertion Nestorius rejects.

35. Ibid., p. 159.

36. P. T. R. Gray, *The Defense of Chalcedon in the East*, Leiden: E. J. Brill, 1979, p. 6. This work is important for much of my argument. It is a relentless assertion that both Nicea and Chalcedon be understood as affirmation of the theological persuasions of Cyril of Alexandria. It is the defense of this theology which allows Justinian to see a "potential solution" for the Church, p. 79.

37. J. Meyendorff, *Christ in Eastern Christian Thought*, Athens: St. Vladimir's, 1975, p. 89.

38. *John Philoponos*, ed. A. Šanda, op. cit., pp. 20-28. The references made to the text of the argument will not follow the pagination but the section and line into which Šanda has divided the chapters of Philoponos. Modern debates about Arius and Athanasius still struggle for consensus.

39. Ibid., p. 24. The Greek text differs from the Syriac in that the relation (σχέσις) is not explicated as one of love (ʾokyt hoḇʾ) but, as we can see, this is indeed the contention of Nestorius.

40. F. M. Young, *From Nicea to Chalcedon*, Philadelphia: Fortress Press, 1983. She writes of Cyril: "... his singlemindedness blinded him to the doubtful morality of the means whereby his ends were achieved," p. 244.

41. H. Chadwick, *The Early Church*, op. cit., p. 194.

42. Ibid., p. 199.

43. W. H. C. Frend, *The Rise of Christianity*, op. cit., p. 761.

44. F. Young, op. cit., pp. 258-63.

45. Nestorius, *The Bazaar of Heracleides*, ed., G. R. Driver, Oxford: Clarendon Press, 1925.

46. Ibid., p. xxxiv.

47. Ibid., p. xxxiv, item vi.

48. Ibid., p. xxxiv, item i.

49. Ibid., p. 154.

50. Ibid., p. 271.

51. Ibid., p. 187.

52. R. L. Wilken, *Judaism and the Early Christian Mind*, New Haven and London: Yale University Press, 1971, pp. 211- 21.

53. Ibid., p. 215.

54. W. H. C. Frend, *Saints and Sinners in the Early Church*, op. cit., pp. 141-56.

55. Ibid., p. 156.

56. P. T. R. Gray, *The Defense of Chalcedon in the East*, Leiden: E. J. Brill, 1979.

57. Cf. T. F. Torrance, *Space, Time, and Incarnation*, Oxford: Oxford University Press, 1969, where the author traces the influence of the concepts of space and time upon dogma in the early Church and in the modern Church. I believe the problem of space defines much of the development of the Church's thinking on the relation of God to the world.

58. H. Chadwick, "Eucharist and Christology in the Nestorian Controversy," in *History and Thought of the Early Church,* op. cit., pp. xvi, 145-64.

59. L. Abramowski and A. E. Goodman, *A Nestorian Collection of Christological Texts*, Cambridge: Cambridge University Press, 1972. I have chosen to discuss *The Twelve Anathema* in the Syriac form because of the work I hope to do with *The Arbiter*. The problem here will be the difficulty of working out 'simultaneity' in the light of God's eternity and the time of Christ.

60. Ibid., pp. 211-18.

61. Ibid., p. 143.

62. Ibid., p. 143, lines 3-14, Nestorius uses b-kyn³ (in nature) ten times, as he distinguishes the union from the kyn³ (nature) of Cyril's Christology.

63. Cf. E. Stump, *De topicis differentiis of Boethius*, Ithaca: Cornell University Press, 1978.

64. L. Abramowski, op. cit., p. 143, lines 10-11.

65. H. Chadwick, *History and Thought of the Early Church*, pp. 146-47.

66. Cf. W. H. C. Frend, *The Rise of Christianity*, op. cit., pp. 766-73, for a short account of the tension in attempting to reach this kind of harmonization between Cyril and the Tome.

67. A. Kerrigan, *St. Cyril of Alexandria*, Rome: Pontificio Instituto Biblico, 1952, claims Cyril employs Θεωρία as in the Platonic tradition (p. 116). The spiritual understanding, however, with which Cyril commonly works is Athanasian and not Platonic because it has nothing to do with the split between theory and sensible experience in Platonic science. Cf. T. F. Torrance, *Transformation and Convergence in the Frame of Knowledge*,

Grand Rapids: Eerdmans, 1984, pp. 63, 89-91, 311-12, for an analysis of the issues here.

68. P. T. R. Gray, *The Defense of Chalcedon in the East*, op. cit., pp. 9-16.

69. Ibid., p. 15. This is another way of grappling with the profound relationality that must exist with us between theory and empirical knowledge. They may not be divorced from one another in any true or real perception of things that are both visible and invisible to us.

70. Ibid., p. 16. The author contends that to see Chalcedon as a victory of Rome and Antioch over Alexandria is to miss the essential nature of Cyril's dominance at the Council.

71. Ibid., p. 5. The author claims we must gain "a deeper understanding of the neglected period between 451 and 553...."

72. W. H. C. Frend, *The Rise of the Monophysite Movement*, op. cit., p. 124.

73. M. G. Fouyas, *The Person of Jesus Christ in the Decisions of the Ecumenical Councils,* Addis Ababa: Central Printing Press, 1976. See especially pp. 58-70, where John Philoponos is identified with the theology of Severus. Cf. M. Moosa, *The Maronites in History*, New York: Syracuse University Press, 1986, pp. 39-63.

74. W. H. C. Frend, *The Rise of the Monophysite Movements*, op. cit., pp. 143-83, and P. T. R. Gray, *The Defense of Chalcedon in the East*, op. cit., pp. 28-33.

75. Frend, ibid., pp. 208-9.

76. Frend, *Saints and Sinners in the Early Church*, op. cit., pp. 157-73. The author continues the perception in the West of Severus as a Monophysitic defender of Cyril's "one incarnate nature."

77. Cf. E. W. Brooks, "A Collection of Letters of Severus of Antioch," PO, ed. R. Graffin and F. Nau, vol. 14, nos. 67-71, Belgique: Editions Brepols, 1973.

78. Ibid., pp. 7-9.

79. Ibid., pp. 10-14.

80. Ibid., pp. 15-20.

81. Ibid., pp. 16-17.

82. Ibid., p. 18.

83. Ibid., pp. 18-20.

84. Ibid., p. 21.

85. Ibid., p. 22.

86. Ibid., pp. 22-29.

87. Ibid., p. 28.

88. Ibid., p. 35.

89. Ibid., p. 36.

90. Ibid., pp. 40-44.

91. Severus refers to Hebrews 1:3 for Christ as the ray of the glory of the Father and the impress of his hypostasis. [ʾytohy gyr ṣmhʾ d-tsḇohth d-ʾḇʾ w-rosmʾ d-qnomh: " for he is the ray of the glory of the Father and the impress of His hypostasis"], p. 8.

92. J. Lebon, *Le Monophysisme Severien*, Lovanii: Universitatis Catholicae Typographus, 1909.

93. Ibid., p. 251.

94. Ibid., pp. 242-62.

95. Ibid., p. 244.

96. Ibid., p. 253.

97. Ibid., p. 297.

98. Ibid., pp. 344-50.

99. Ibid., p. 304. I associate the concept of 'pleonastic' relations with the struggle for 'complementarity' in modern science.

100. Ibid., p. 242, footnote 2.

101. Frend, *Saints and Sinners in the Early Church,* p. 168.

102. Gray, op. cit., repeatedly strives to make this point throughout his argument. It is interesting to note that in this light he never makes mention of John Philoponos.

103. This assessment is repeated by R. V. Sellers, *The Council of Chalcedon*, London: SPCK, 1961, where it is asserted that Justinian would deny the Nestorian interpretation of Leo's Tome, and by R. C. Chestnut, *Three Monophysite Christologies*, London: Oxford University Press, 1976, where Severus is understood to find psychologically odious the idea that Christ acted now divinely, when he cast out demons, and then humanly, when he wept and prayed.

104. J. Meyendorff, *Christ in Eastern Christian Thought*, Athens: St. Vladimir's Seminary Press, 1975, p. 80.

105. H. Chadwick, *The Early Church*, op. cit., p. 208. See pp. 200-12 for an excellent short history of the struggle and fate of Justinian's efforts.

106. J. Meyendorff, "Justinian, the Empire and the Church," DOP, 22 (1968), pp. 45-60.

107. The most recent studies assert that the claim of the divinity of Christ is the source in fact of many of Justinian's problems in governing. Cf. C. E. Gunton, *Yesterday and Today*, Grand Rapids: Eerdmans, 1983, pp. 189-90.

108. Meyendorff, op. cit., p. 48.

109. Ibid., p. 52. Cf. H. Chadwick, *Boethius*, op. cit., p. 189. "To Justinian their programme offered high possibilities for that reconciliation of the churches which was close to the emperor's heart."

110. H. Chadwick, *Boethius*, op. cit., pp. 185-90.

111. Ibid., p. 180.

112. Ibid., p. 189.

113. Ibid., pp. 191-92.

114. Ibid., p. 191. Perhaps the split between the intelligible and the experiential dimensions of the world confound the issues about the term 'nature' in most all of the debates.

115. Ibid., p. 192.

116. Ibid., pp. 193-94.

117. Ibid., p. 194. "The priority of an individual to his accidents is forgotten."

118. Cf. also M. Gibson, "The Opuscula Sacra in the Middle Ages," in *Boethius,* Oxford: Blackwell, 1981, pp. 214- 34.

119. Cf. T. F. Torrance, "Truth and Authority in the Church," in *Transformation and Convergence in the Frame of Knowledge*, op. cit., pp. 311-12.

120. H. Chadwick, *Boethius*, op. cit., pp. 195-96.

121. Ibid., p. 220.

122. Ibid., pp. 46-56.

123. Ibid., pp. 29-45. Professor Chadwick entitles this section "The hard road to church unity."

124. Frend, *Saints and Sinners*, op. cit., p. 172. M. Moosa, *The Maronites in History*, op. cit., discusses the letters accusing Severus of the brutal murders of Chalcedonian monks.

125. H. Martin, "Jean Philopon et la controverse tritheite du VIe siècle," SP, vol. V (1962), pp. 519-25. ". . . en effet, Jean Philopon cite son Diatêtês, dans un ouvrage qu'il composa contre Chalcedoine au moment même

ou se tenait à Constantinople le Ve Concile (des Trois Chapters), ce qui implique que le Diatêtês parut en tout cas avant 553, tandis que Jean ne fit son apparition que 3 ou 4 plus tard et mourut, nous l'avons dit, vers 565."

126. Gray, op. cit., p. 154.

127. Diehl, op. cit., pp. 364-66, 661-62.128. Gray, op. cit., pp. 157-58.

129. Meyendorff, *Christ in Eastern Christian Thought*, op. cit., p. 89.

130. Meyendorff, op. cit., DOP, 22 (1982), p. 58.

131. J. Philoponos, "Letter to Justinian," in *Opuscula Monophysitica*, ed. A. Sanda, London, 1930. I will give my translation of this letter in chapter four, with comments relative to the theological issues it addresses.

132. Meyendorff, DOP, 22 (1982), p. 60.

133. J. Philoponos, *The Arbiter*, in *Opuscula Monophysitica*, op. cit., chapter 1.

"This attempt by Alexandrian theologians to think through and set on a sound scientific basis the Christian understanding of the relation of God to the world had a far-reaching impact on the foundations of philosophy and science, as one can see, for example, when the relational view of space and time was carried over by John Philoponos in the sixth century from theology into physics."

T. F. Torrance, *Reality and Scientific Theology*, p. 5

"The oblivion into which Philoponus' works have fallen is deplorable as they contain not a few incisive remarks which show how the doctrine of creation could inspire scientifically fruitful reflections about the physical world."

S.L. Jaki, *Cosmos and Creator,* p. 68

CHAPTER THREE

JOHN PHILOPONOS AND THE SCIENTIFIC CULTURE OF ALEXANDRIA

The year AD 529 was, Richard Sorabji has written, "annus mirabilis" for Christianity.[1] St. Benedict is said to have founded the monastery at Monte Cassino, Justinian closed the Platonic Academy at Athens, the Council of Orange is supposed to have settled matters about God and the free will of the race, and John Philoponos, in the Academy at Alexandria, published *De aeternitate mundi* against Proclus, the first serious attack from a Christian point of view upon the habitual propensity of the ancient Greek mind to think the cosmos was eternal. It had only been two years since Justinian's enthronement, but the Serbian born Emperor's policy of uniting the Empire under the Pantocrator was already being felt. The closure of the Athenian School, seen by some as a threat to intellectual freedom, should not, however, be understood as an imperial policy against the university's commitment to higher education. It can be shown that Justinian did not move against philosophy or science when he denied support to Athens, but against pagan worship of stars and their celestial angels.[2] He opposed pagan superstitions, not the rational investigation of the nature of the cosmos. At the great Academy in Alexandria, perhaps become the Church's unwanted answer to Tertullian's rhetorical question about Jerusalem and Athens, John Philoponos was effectual in passing on the lectures of Ammonius, son of Hermias, as well as his own arguments, to students who would one day teach at Constantinople, under the Imperial Seal, a full range of studies inherited from the great intellectual traditions of the ancient world.[3] Justinian stood for the great scientific tradition at Alexandria, deeply rooted in the history of a city whose wonders had made her in the East the center of a commerce unrivaled in the world. E. A. Parsons can write of her:[4]

> Other cities are but the cities of the country around them;
> Alexandria is the city of the world.

In BC 332, Alexander of Macedon was greeted by Egyptians as their deliverer from Persian oppression. At Memphis, he was declared a god and he founded at a small ancient village named Rhakotis, nestled nicely between the Nile, the Mareotic Lake, and the Mediterranean Sea, the city of Alexandria.[5] The city was destined from its founding to become "the greatest emporium of the inhabited world,"[6] the mercantile capital of a melting pot of peoples among the land of the Pharaohs, and the center in Late Antiquity of classical Greek education. She was "a nursing mother for men of every nation."[7] The dynasties of the Ptolemies made her the capital of Egyptian power, displacing ancient Memphis, within the Greek and Roman Empires.[8]

Even though little remains of her past glory today, Alexandria became famed throughout the ancient world for her Lighthouse, a beacon in her busy harbor, considered one of the seven wonders, capable from a height of some 400 feet of guiding mariners into her ports. Her trade and commerce was without equal. She became the grain supply of the Empire. But most importantly for our study, she provided the means by which at her library the greatest collection of manuscripts in the history of the ancient world could be established. Every book that was brought onto her docks was copied afresh for its owner, and the original retained for the great Museum of Alexandria. There in midst of ancient gods and temples was accumulated the intellectual achievement of the race. Farrington has written of it:[9]

> The Museum which the Ptolemies founded and maintained in
> Alexandria rapidly became the centre of a scientific movement
> that might have transformed antiquity into a semblance of the
> modern world.

Supported by the Dynasties, it was there that Euclid (300 BC) wrote his El-ements, the foundation of geometrical logics which would serve for all time as a basis for the application of measurement to physical reality. Apollonius (240 BC) developed for the Ptolemaic Cosmology the epicycles for the motions of the heavenly bodies, necessary to explain the discovery by Hipparchus (125 BC) of precessional movements of the equinoxes, scientific data which were used in order to deny the heliocentric theory of Aristarchus (287 BC).[10]

The heavens were not alone open to this heuristic aspect of ancient Greek empiricism, but Herophilus did research on the brain and Erasistratus studied the blood, establishing the first medical schools (240 BC). Archimedes (285 BC) agreed with Aristarchus against Aristotle and wrote mechanics based upon a heliocentric cosmos. Eratosthenes, in the same century, was summoned from Athens to Alexandria by Ptolemaios III to educate his successor, and while at the Museum measured the circumference of the earth (within 2 percent of modern values of 24,989 miles at the equator).[11] By 220 BC, Alexandria had replaced Athens as the center of culture in the development of the civilization. Farrington writes:[12]

> At Alexandria the resources of a powerful state were for the first time put behind the scientists, and where advance was possible it was made with astonishing rapidity.

Certainly the beacon of Pharos at Alexandria had drawn into its light the creative genius of the race, where a royal society provided that atmosphere which was necessary for the progress of civilization. It has not been easy for scholars to understand why Greek science suddenly ceased its creative development. Bell writes typically in his article on Alexandria:[13]

> Only the curious deadness and dessication which fell upon the Greek genius a little before the beginning of the Christian era prevented the Greeks from anticipating many of the marvels of modern science and led to the neglect of those already discovered.

Many feel that the empirical interests of Democritus and Aristotle became overshadowed by Neoplatonic efforts to harmonize them with Socrates and Plato, introducing into the scientific method unnecessary metaphysical elements which tended to kill true science.[14] This is exemplified in the works of Plotinus, Iamblichus, and Proclus, in which a kind of Gnosticism is embedded in the purpose of the cosmos, in which there rages an intellectual struggle of the human soul to reach eternal essences.[15] Richard Sorabji can record the opinion that Justinian's closure of Athens was not so much a defeat of a vibrant body of knowledge as a burial of a "corpse," the result of the killing of creative science by a mania for those kinds of metaphysical speculations which imprison the possibilities of free discovery with magical powers and supernatural phenomena.[16]

The Benedictine scholar, Stanley Jaki, claims that Greek science had already lost its creativity by the time the Museum opened in Alexandria,[17] a failure marked by the domination of Stoic philosophy and the suffocation of the genius of the race in an atomistic reductionism capable of thinking of the All as the mechanical flux of numbers of atoms, free from any metaphysical considerations.[18] Jaki has argued, in a number of works in fact, for the recognition that both a kind of reductionism upwards, inherent to the division between the eternality and the divinity of the heavens and the temporality and mortality of the nature of earth, and the atomistic reductionism downwards, intrinsic to the mechanical nature of things, must be seen as capable of entrapping the race in false assumptions about the scientific method.[19] Like

Sorabji, Jaki will often point to John Philoponos as the example of a man who, in seeking to avoid these reductionisms, attempted with a creative vitality far beyond the "corpse" of Athens to keep alive in Alexandria the possibility and the significance of scientific methodology and discovery in the world. Embodied in his voluminous works is the proof that the Alexandrian tradition in philosophy and science had not completely deteriorated into an encyclopaedic character. His effort, in fact, is coming to be understood as a revolutionary endeavor, with the force of an individual mind whose creative genius was truly pioneering, capable of the possibility of harmonizing with the truth of the Creator the truth of his creatures in the orders and structures of the creation.[20] We will have to come to terms with this effort if we are going to appreciate the life-setting of *The Arbiter*. For it appears manifestly evident that the Christology of *The Arbiter* cannot be understood divorced from the cosmology of the brilliant Alexandrian scientist. About the same year that Albert Einstein had published his epoch-making advance with relativity theory,[21] the modern scientific community had begun to recognize this contribution of John Philoponos. Emil Wöhwill pointed to him as the forerunner in the ancient world to the development in physics associated with Copernicus, Galileo, and Isaac Newton.[22] The Grammarian is understood to have been able to overcome some of the fundamental assumptions inherent to the Ptolemaic cosmology and Aristotelian physics developed by Neoplatonism, and to conceive of physical theory in such a way that not until the acceptance of Newton's gravitation could his ideas be given the credit they deserved. Wöhwill wrote:[23]

> Und hier ist ein Kommentator aus den Anfang des 6. Jahrhunderts, der Satz für Satz den Aristoteles widerlegt, seine Trugschlüsse offenbart und Anschauungen zur Geltung bringt, zu denen die führenden Geister des 16. Jahrhunderts sich bekennen.

In 1927 George Sarton echoed this evaluation of the Alexandrian. He gave the name of John Philoponos a landmark significance in the development of scientific culture,[24] and saw the need for a general study of the scientist, citing his originality in opposing Aristotelian views of motion and his influence on Arabic and Jewish philosophers in the Middle Ages.[25] Pierre Duhem's monumental history of scientific thought mentions Philoponos no less than 59 times.[26] Correcting early mistakes about the dates of his life,[27] Duhem shows how precocious were his ideas of space and time, much opposed by his contemporary Simplicius, who could be astonished at Philoponos' irreverent use of Aristotle, and also his kinetic theory against the Master's idea of the motion in the world (ἀντιπερίστασις), associated with Aristotle's effort to find natural purpose in the cosmos.[28] They are found influencing Al Gaza¯li, the Muslim <u>mutakallim</u> who defended the concept of the beginning of space and time against Arabic arguments for Aristotle's notion of the eternity of the world.[29] Thomas Aquinas and John Duns Scotus are both acquainted with the ideas of Philoponos through this influence.[30] Duhem can write of the contribution of Philoponos:[31]

> ... Jean d'Alexandrie, dit le Chre'tien, meriterait d'e`tre compte ou nombre des grand ge'nies de l'Antiquite', d'etre celebre comme un des principaux precursers de la Science moderne.

Taton's *History of Science* has noted the original views achieved by the scientist in ancient Alexandria, again pointing to his impetus theory of motion against Aristotle's ideas about the nature of motion.[32] And in 1967, Walter Böhm answered Sarton's call for a comprehensive general study.[33]

There is actually very little known of the personal life of John the Alexandrian Grammarian called Philoponos. His birth can only be estimated at sometime between AD 475 and 495, and it is also debated whether it was in Caesarea or Alexandria.[34] Early scholarship translated his name "lover of work" and some thought it was an acquired name due to the voluminous character of his manuscripts, but since then we know it was because of his membership in a Christian group that was known for its zealousness.[35] His Christian conversion in his youth is also debated, as well as its effect on his scientific works.[36] There is no indication he was ever married, and one gets an impression of him as a highly disciplined believer who committed the entirety of his life to Christ and the investigation of the cosmos as Christ's creation with an amazing singularity of will, intention, and industry. Ammonius, at any rate, appointed him his successor at the Academy in Alexandria and, even though Simplicius can mock his office of Grammarian as inferior to that of the Philosopher, he was probably, when Justinian began to reign, the most renowned scientist of his day.[37] There is little doubt that he was the foremost commentator on the works of Aristotle in his time.[38] Joannou calls him the first Christian to attempt to achieve a completely adequate philosophical system.[39] Böhm, in fact, compares him to Aristotle and Galen in his empirical freedom from Socratic and Platonic metaphysics.[40] His attack upon Proclus in AD 529 is that of a man who was confident of his resolution of the problem of the intelligible and the sensible so central to the development of scientific thought.[41] At the heart of his argument with Proclus and Simplicius lies his belief in the Church's doctrine of creation out of nothing. It allowed him to conceive a theory of motion of which Böhm writes:[42]

> Was Archimedes für die mechanische Statik leistete, das vollzog Philoponos, freilich bei weitem nicht mit derselben Endgültigkeit und Vollendung, für die Dynamik.

It is impossible, claims Böhm, to understand this development of thought while attempting to isolate metaphysical concepts from those ideas by which he attempts to apprehend the nature of physical reality. The Alexandrian Scientist must be seen as both an experimentalist and a theorist who was free to call even the masters of the philosophical tradition to task over the Truth.[43] Although he could agree with Aristotle on one level of his thought, especially on an empirical or phenomenological one, he could argue adamantly against him over the way God indeed was to be thought related to the cosmos and its physics.[44]

The result is not only a new impetus theory of motion, but a field theory of light which attempted to apprehend both its bodily character and its incorporeal energy. This theory allowed Philoponos to conceive of a resolution to the problem of the whole and the parts in Greek thought which will not separate the intelligible from the sensible, the theoretical from the phenomenal, but permits him to think them together in a dynamic way in which the subject-object relation is open to the creative, providential activity of the Pantokrator.[45] This meant that the Grammarian would have nothing to do with Aristotle's divine heavens and its fifth essence,[46] the kind of blasphemy which enraged Simplicius against him. In this development of his thought, Böhm is able to show how the Episcopate tradition in Alexandria greatly influenced Philoponos. It is understood that the Grammarian belongs to the effort, begun most comprehensively by Athanasius, made by the Church Fathers, Basil the Great (329-379), Gregory of Nyssa (331-395), and later Cyril of Alexandria and Severus of Antioch, to think together as consistently as possible the meaning of the Incarnation of the Logos of God, the Eternal Son, with the Church's Doctrine of Creation. The genius of Philoponos is appreciated when we realize that he is not only forerunner in the ancient world to Copernicus, Galileo, and Newton, but that he was also known to and deeply appreciated by a scientist like Huygens.[47] So great was his ability to invent creatively a synthesis of the invisible and visible worlds, the intangible with the tangible, and by means of it to point us to that kind of objectivity with which we might grasp the real world and its relation to our perceptions of it! It is interesting to note in this respect that, although Philoponos had a running feud with Christians who wanted to read the Bible in some literal manner and who could also think that the world was in some manner eternal, at least in the mind of God, he was unwilling to divorce Biblical Truth from cosmological truth. Evidently, he could even claim that whatever Plato and Aristotle were able to think that was true about the world was grounded in the prophets of Israel.[48] This kind of affirmation, not generally accepted by modern exegetes, posits what Böhm calls a "Konkordanztheorie."[49] Although the Bible is not meant to provide scientific knowledge of the universe, and allows man a freedom and a duty to investigate the cosmos and to discover its truths, there must exist some reason (Vernunft) and scientific explanation (Erfahrungswissenschaft) for the relation created by God between the Creator and the creation. It is Böhm's belief that such a concordance-theory would prove helpful to modern readers of the Bible, so that cosmological and eschatological considerations are not cut off and divorced from theological truth, as if the Bible were meant purely for "spiritual" realities divorced from the creation itself. For this reason, he writes:[50]

> Für Philoponos war das noch verhältnismäßig einfach, weil das damalige Weltbild mit dem der Bibel doch noch konformer war.

Here the intelligible world and the empirical world are thought together according to their natures. It is this belief that drives the thinking of John Philoponos, and must be understood as the ground behind his argument in *The Arbiter*.

In spite of this recognition, it remains true that the scholary world has been slow to translate the works of Philoponos and to make available for the many in Western civilization an opportunity to consider the significance of his various writings. Only a few fragments have found their way into English. Cohen and Drabkin have studied the commentaries of Philoponos against Aristotle's concept of antiperistasis.[51] They provide translations of fragments of Philoponos' *Commentary on Aristotle's Physics* [678.24-684-10 (Vitelli)], in which the Alexandrian Scientist writes:[52]

> For Aristotle wrongly assumes that the ratio of the times required for motion through various media is equal to the ratio of the densities of the media...

(Here Philoponos seems to intuit the gravitational concept of Galileo) and in another place he writes:[53]

> Rather is it necessary to assume that some incorporeal motive force is imparted by the projector to the projectile, and that the air set in motion contributes either nothing at all or else very little to this motion of the projectile.

Thus, he conceives of an impetus theory of motion in place of the antiperistasis theory of Aristotle. In these passages Philoponos displays his ability to analyze empirical data in light of a theory and, depending upon its ability to "satisfy our minds," accept or reject it. When an unacceptable theory is rejected, then he posits one that does satisfy the mind about the phenomena. Clagett, who like Armstrong associates the Christian conversion of the Grammarian with failing intellectual powers and takes Justinian's move against Athens as a "rebuff" of scientific activity in the sixth century, is also concerned with Philoponos' impetus theory.[54] He marks the rise in recent years of the stature of John as a natural philosopher, and interestingly is aware of the Syriac Christians of Jundi-Shapur and Edessa, where it seems plausible that Philoponos' writings may have been translated into Syriac. Perhaps some disciple of Sergius of Reshaina (AD 536), a Monophysite priest and physician, is the source of the extant copy of *The Arbiter*.[55]

Shmuel Sambursky, who detects in Philoponos "... the reasoning of a man carried away by his revolutionary zeal and the momentum of a new and irresistible conception," asserts that the arguments mounted by the Alexandrian scientist were absolutely unique in the history of scientific ideas.[56] He contends that, among the three thousand pages of John's scientific works, one finds again and again passages of "great brilliance" and "originality and ingenuity and acute and independent criticism."[57] Drawing upon his belief in the creation of the world and a thorough knowledge of Aristotelian and Neoplatonic thought, Philoponos uncovered evident contradictions in their conceptions and from every conceivable point attacked the idea of the eternity of the cosmos and the Ptolemaic Universe's divorce of the heavens and the earth, the intelligible and the sensible. In so doing, Philoponos is seen to explicate the real contingency of the world. Sambursky translates from fragments quoted by Simplicius in his efforts to deny the cogency of John's arguments:[58]

> One could concede for instance that the celestial bodies, being held together by the divine will, will not perish; this, however, would not exclude that by their specific nature they are subject to the law of destruction.

Heaven and the whole universe were created in a physical form and thus also presuppose a privation out of which they were created and into which they perish.

For Philoponos, the doctrine of creation implied the real contingency of the cosmos, which meant that the world was dependent upon God for what it was as an independent nature sustained in its form and matter by the divine power of the creative will of the Creator. The idea was blasphemous to Simplicius, and he records what he dislikes.[59] All things generated by nature one out of another are equally subject to a beginning of their existence. Each species--and this particularly holds for the primary elements--must have a first member which derived its origin not from a similar or dissimilar one preceding it, but was created by God together with the formation of the universe. The idea that in any beginning we must leave room in our thinking for a divine freedom, alongside of a temporal aspect, was not intelligible to Simplicius and even many Christians. Simplicius claimed the cosmos of the Grammarian was deterministic and mechanical atheism,[60] and we shall have to discuss the concept of the contingency of the world further as we attempt to appreciate the full range of the thought of Philoponos. Sambursky also shows how John conceived of space differently from Aristotle, whose container notion assigned to it an absolutely passive quality. Philoponos, however, gave it a power of its own:[61]

> Space is not the boundary of the containing body, as one can well conclude from the fact that it has a certain extension in three dimensions, different from the bodies placed in it, incorporeal according to its proper nature and nothing but the empty interval of a body--in fact, space and the void are the same by their nature....
>
> And I do not maintain that this extension either is or can be empty of every body. This is never the case, for though the void in its proper sense is different from the bodies placed in it, as I said before, space is never devoid of bodies, just as we say that matter differs from form, but yet can never be devoid of form.

Here a relational view of space, grounded in the concept of the contingency of the cosmos, which is created in both its form and matter, is explicated. Likewise, since time is a created thing and absolutely distinguished from eternity, it is not infinite but relationally bound up with the motion of matter and the measure of it. Space and time are not, therefore, independent aspects of the cosmos, but profoundly bound up with the very nature of the structures of the universe.[62] Sambursky also translates, as an example of this method of thought, a long passage by Philoponos on the relationship of sweetness and color in a mixture of honey, to the end that he says:[63]

> This is the only case on record in antiquity of the qualitative treatment of a functional relationship, and it goes to show how the development of a concept of supreme importance for science was held up for lack of a suitable method of description--in this case graphical representation.

Sambursky summarizes the relation of Aristotle and Philoponos by declaring that, wherever he can, the Grammarian will honor the Master, but he shows great maturity when he is compelled to argue against him.[64] The attack upon the dichotomies intrinsic to Aristotle's physics and the Ptolemaic Universe showed a striking scientific imagination, disciplined by empirical methods but free to invent new analogies and concepts that would penetrate more deeply into the real nature of things.[65] Simplicius' objections and anger pale now in the light of modern thought, but when one thinks of John's running battle with Kosmos Indikopleustes, with his student Elias, who never embraced the concept of the contingency of the world, along with Simplicius, one feels Philoponos faced as much anathema against his scientific work as we know he was to face with the writing of *The Arbiter*. Even Sambursky can say that his later work, *De opificio mundi*, displays a submission to dogmas and a loss of the intellectual boldness that once marked the scientist. Yet it is evident that he had already done more than enough to secure a place in the history of scientific thought. When we appreciate in a proper perspective the cogency of the arguments for the fundamental insights he possessed into the nature of space and time, matter and energy, and light itself, we must admit:[66]

> The unique position of Philoponos in the history of scientific ideas is given by the fact that through him a confrontation of scientific cosmology and monotheism took place for the first time.

Because of him, it is impossible to go on contending that the development of Christianity spelled the end of Greek science. To the contrary, Sambursky has written:[67]

> One is tempted to speculate on how the course of the history of ideas would have changed had the doctrine of Philoponus been accepted by the Church instead of the Aristotelian conception.

That these ideas have been and are being vindicated by modern science is the source of Sambursky's temptation.

In her Ph.D. dissertation at the History of Science department of Harvard University, Jean Christensen has focused her attention upon Philoponos' theory of light over against Aristotle's ideas of transparent mediums.[68] Although I believe she does not sufficiently take into consideration Philoponos' concept of the contingency of the world, nor penetrates into the significance of how the concept is employed in the debate between Chalcedonian and the neo-Chalcedonian parties of Justinian's Empire, her study does demonstrate how Philoponos could make skillful use of Aristotelian concepts while introducing fundamentally unique ideas into the way we are to relate our understanding to physical realities. With his contemplation of light, the scientific method (κατά φύσιν) learned from Ammonius at the Academy, along with his commitment to think together the tangible and the intangible, Philoponos developed a conception of the most subtle kind of matter and incorporeal energy. Aristotle had considered light to be an attribute of a transparent medium, with the result that he thought light rays were originated with the human eye. But for Philoponos, bodies could receive light because of its incorporeal energy and transmit it according to geometrical optics. Light is not associated with rays from the eye.[69] Light was to the eye as heat is to skin or sound to the ear. It is propagated by a succession of effects which appear to be instantaneous but, unlike sound, does not require a medium in which to travel. Philoponos was, in fact, applying his impetus theory to light so that he overcame, while saving the appearances, the trap of the categories of Aristotle, where light is compared to freezing, an alteration of the state of something capable of transparency.[70] I believe the ambiguities in Christensen's analysis of Philoponos' theory of light are bound up with the question of the eternity of the world and the contingency of the world. She does not seem to recognize that Philoponos, because of the doctrine of creation, would not embrace the Nous of Neoplatonic or Stoic thought as the necessary cause of the impetus force empowering light movement.[71] Sambursky is helpful here.[72] Appreciating the boldness and originality of John's approach, he understands that the scientist rejected a strictly mechanical view of the propagation of the incorporeal energy of light and has grounded his thought in an original impetus whose force is contingently related to the room we must make in our thinking for a divine freedom in any beginning. He admires the struggle of Philoponos to free himself from "formal preservation of a time-honored terminology" in order to relate his thought accordingly to the actual way in which the nature of a thing presents itself to us.[73] Perhaps it needs to be said here that, for Philoponos, this means that light was what it was because of an uncreated rationality to which no causality in the physics of Aristotle could be related, and language must somehow bear the ability to point us to this divine freedom rather than any first cause of a series of causes in the cosmos.

Recognizing the work of Sambursky, Robert Todd has attempted to broaden our appreciation of the Alexandrian scientist.[74] The originality and the force of his arguments relative to light, mass, dynamics, space, and time cannot be denied. But Todd would show us how Philoponos was able, within the Aristotelian tradition, to conceive repeatedly unique ideas whose fruitfulness may not be yet fully appreciated. He utilizes parts of *de anima* and *de generatione et corruptione*, works based directly upon the lectures of Ammonius, and *Physics* and *Meteorologic*, both of which, because they contain arguments against the eternity of the world, are considered to reflect Christianity.[75] Todd rehearses some of the infinity arguments employed by Philoponos to argue for a beginning of the universe against Aristotle's eternity, and tries to show how the ancient debate, raging throughout Philoponos' tenure at the Academy, was won by the Grammarian because he treated time in the same way as other commentaries treated matter.[76] Philoponos used Aristotle against himself to overcome the habit of mind that associates forever with eternity, and was not merely interested in a theory of infinite sets.[77]

But Philoponos could also insist that form and matter together were involved in the unique nature of things and were not randomly structured. Infinite divisibility, which Aristotle championed, was not really possible. Todd sees the potential here in Philoponos for a quantitative science of mixtures or chemical reactions, developed by modern atomic structure, but notes that the Alexandrian never took this step. He also points out that the scientist opposed Aristotle's view that soul was present in the male sperm in favor of a "complete creation."[78] In medicine, Philoponos could be just as original or individual even as a part of the philosophical traditions which were the Academy at Alexandria.[79]

Richard Walzer has written a magisterial article on the influence of John Philoponos upon Arabic thought, and can see the Grammarian as a Muslim dialectical theologian.[80] Al-Ghazālī used his arguments against Al-Fārābī and Avicenna and was followed later by Al-Kindi. Though we know next to nothing about how the ideas of Philoponos came to be preserved in the Syriac, so that 250 years later the <u>mutakallimun</u> could employ them in their debates about the nature of the world, their influence is undeniable. The main issues revolve around the concept of contingency. Aristotle treated that which was true and real, and yet contingent, only as accidentals with which scientific knowledge was not ultimately concerned.[81] But John Philoponos disagreed and insisted that, however difficult it was for us, contingent things were the object of scientific attention since we would know things in the way they compel themselves upon our knowing of them ($\kappa\alpha\tau\grave{\alpha}$ $\tau\grave{\eta}\nu$ $\phi\upsilon\sigma\iota\kappa\grave{\eta}\nu$ $\delta\acute{\upsilon}\nu\alpha\mu\iota\nu$). This was, again, the fundamental principle for the scientific method in the Alexandrian Academy. Without it, God's world is not properly investigated, since it is in its entirety a created and contingent reality which has been given by the Creator a nature which is not self-explanatory, a truth that does not lead necessarily back to a first cause that possesses a formal and logical relationship with its effects. In this, Walzer realizes, John Philoponos challenged the most cherished and fundamental tenets of all Greek philosophy.[82] He writes:[83]

> Nature, as analyzed and understood by Aristotle and the Neoplatonists, and the realm of the Christian God belong to different domains of reality; in the same way Greek philosophy and the Hebrew faith are by no means one and the same thing. The laws which apply to the activity of nature are not laws which can limit the omnipotence of God. John Philoponos does not deny (nor does Al-Kindi—as shown above, p. 188) that nature actually produces new things out of previously existing things (*Simpl. Phys.* p. 1145, 7ff.); God is different in as far as he can create new things out of nothing (*Phys.* p. 1145, 9).

The divine freedom means the eternal power to establish the world with- in an independence whose nature is in its created freedom ultimately dependent upon the power of the free creative will of God. In this sense, there is no nec-

essary relation between God and the nature of the cosmos, but a free and di-

vinely sustaining one which is not like any of the generation found within it.

The duration and existence of the universe can only point us away from itself

to what is not generated and what is not contingent.[84] Walzer writes:[85]

> This amounts in the case of John Philoponos to being able to
> write in the time honored way of the philosophers and
> commentators on Plato and Aristotle (who would correspond to
> the Islamic philosophers) and to master at the same time the
> systems of thought developed by the Christian patristic authors
> such as St. Basil or Gregory of Nyssa (who would be similar to the
> mainly apologistic Mutakallīmun).

In this development of thought, the human imagination was assigned relation-

al responsibility, along with the other faculties, in the struggle to achieve

that concordance between reason and perception which would allow one to

save the appearances with a mode of rationality appropriate to the way

things actually had been made to be.[86] Imagination ($\phi\alpha\nu\tau\acute{\alpha}\sigma\iota\alpha$) guarded against

any mania in this process by the commitment of the human will to apprehend

the realities of the cosmos according to the way truth presented itself to us.

This meant for John Philoponos, unlike Boethius in Rome, that there was no

divine spark in the soul of the race, by which we might ascend to the divine

light. All created reality in its form and matter, including man in his soul and

body, was contingent being whose nature was both independent of and bound

up with the nature of a loving and good God.[87]

But admittedly, the works of Philoponos remain accessible to us only

in the fragments provided by these scholars and Richard Sorabji has recog-

nized the need to provide a fuller presentation of them. In 1983, Sorabji

served as director of a conference of international scholars gathered at the

Institute of Classical Studies of London University.[88] It was the beginning of an attempt to get more of the works of Philoponos before the English-speaking world and to achieve a more complete understanding of their contribution to the development of thought. The participants were Sorabji, David Furley of Princeton, Philippe Hoffman of Paris, Michael Wolff of Bielefeld, Henry Blumenthal of Liverpool, and Henry Chadwick of Cambridge. They attempted to explore the entire range of the significance of John Philoponos. In his opening address, Sorabji argued, against the common idea that philosophy after the third century AD suffered a loss of creative vitality, that Philoponos should be considered a turning point in the history of thought. Utilizing fundamental concepts implied by creatio ex nihilo and a surprisingly thorough knowledge of Aristotle and the Neoplatonic effort to harmonize the Master with the metaphysics of Plato, Philoponos argued successfully against the pagan notions of the eternity of the world and the separation of the heavens and the intelligible world from the earth and the sensible world. This meant, among other things, a conception of space as a function of the energy and matter of the cosmos rather than the container notion or the receptacle concept of Plato and Aristotle. Space played an active role in the way matter appeared in the universe, all of which could not be divorced from time. With Sambursky,[89] it is to be understood that infinite space is not an actuality and the universe may not be infinite in either space or time. Philoponos opposed the atomists, and the temptation to reduce the regularities in the orders of creation down into a purely mechanical system, on the grounds of a rejection of the infinite. Creation is a unique and contingent reality which may not be apprehended by any form of reductionism, either upwards into eternal forms or downwards into mechanical ones. Sorabji insisted that the arguments of Philoponos make it plain, since even Bonaventure and Kant are but reflections of their cogency, that philosophy was far from dead in 529 AD. David Furley wrestled with the idea of extension in the space of Philoponos. Since place has beginning inseparable from matter, and extension (διάστημα) without substance (ὀυσίος), but with magnitude (ποσὸν), it is a logical absurdity according to Aristotle. But we must realize that the nature of things does not necessarily follow after our hypotheses about appearances, and that, in fact, it is possible for created reality to possess both matter and magnitude whose substance and form belong beyond them. For Philoponos, the cosmos must be conceived to be one complex and dynamic reality whose invariant character and motion are bound up in contingent relations with one another, inseparable in form and matter. The problem of translating διάστημα is real because of the contingent nature of the relation between matter and space. The διάστημα that belongs to the place of matter and the διάστημα that belongs to incorporeal space are profoundly related but cannot mean exactly the same thing.[90] Space and place and extension must be on one level of reality the same thing and yet on another quite distinguishable, a good reminder to us of the way language must point away from itself to actual things if it is to be understood properly. The fact that Philoponos could use διάστημα for both dimensions of created reality must be taken seriously in the dynamics of the world he investigates in the way he does. Certainly, it means that he has rejected completely Aristotle's container notion of space as a receptacle in which the motion of the matter of the cosmos occurs. For Philoponos, somehow we must conceive of the universe as both finite and unbounded in its space, time, and matter. His concept of its tri-dimensionality is the category he employed to think together the invisible and visible aspects of created reality.

The dynamical forces of such a world were surveyed by Michael Wolff. I have already discussed the nature of contingent cause as in opposition to the First Cause in Aristotelian physics, and this is understood to present us with an unique kind of necessity by which the impetus theory of Philoponos is consistently thought throughout the entire nature of the cosmos. As such, in opposition to the inertial system inherent to the receptacle view of space, it is causally related in a creative freedom to the divine freedom of the Creator. In Philoponos' cosmos, freedom, spontaneity, and contingent causality are profoundly related, so that even the soul of the body or the body of the soul of man participates in its energy. This means that even our notions of free will must be uniquely understood to be limited by the freedom God possesses to create freely a relationship of His Being with the creation. Wolff suggests that even ethical authority should find its legitimate ground in these kinds of dynamics.

Dr. Hoffmann attempted to explore the animosity towards Philoponos that was shown by his colleague in Athens, Simplicius. It is felt that with good reason, in view of Justinian's move against Athens and his fondness for Philoponos and the Alexandrian Academy, Simplicius was bitter against the Grammarian. But Simplicius' disgust with John, whom he never met, is based more upon his reverence for Aristotle and Plato and the sacredness of the traditions which had for years and years attempted to harmonize the renowned philosophers. His hatred of the Alexandrian is finally a religious act, one which will not tolerate the blasphemous and ephemeral character of thought of a simple Grammarian. Hoffmann translates him as he invokes even King David against the Τἐχῖνος:[92]

> I think that this individual, whoever he is, has a degenerate sensory faculty, since he thinks of the light of the heavens and that of glow worms to be similar or identical. In his headlong search for vainglory, he has not noticed that he is aligning himself with a party opposed to the famous David's, whom he honors above all. For David shows that he does not imagine celestial beings to be of the same nature as sublunary ones, when he says, "The heavens declare the glory of God and the firmament showeth his handiwork." The heavens and the firmament--not glow worms and fish scales!

Thus could the sacredness of the Ptolemaic Cosmology, the one inherited by the great Dante, be invoked!

Professor Chadwick presented a survey of the theological works by Philoponos, with an extended look at *The Arbiter*. He sees the work as a cool analysis of the controversy between Chalcedonians and Monophysites over the unity of the God-Man, Christ. The debate over the phrase "in two natures" of Leo's Tome, which Dioscorus could not accept at Chalcedon, and the phrase "of two natures," common to Cyril's Christology, had so wracked Christendom and haunted Justinian that he turned for some progress to Philoponos. *The Arbiter* attempted to reconcile the parties in the debate with a discussion of the unity of Christ from within the scientific tradition at the Academy of Alexandria. Thus, he claims, Neoplatonic terms are used in an attempt to define the "single composite nature" of the Person of Christ. John's conclusion that "of" was better than "in" was never a compelling argument and could save no one from "soiling the conscience." Justinian's attempt to appease the Monophysites by condemning the *Three Chapters* of Theodore of Mopsuestia and his disciples along with a neo-Chalcedonian symbol whose definition of the faith assured a Cyrillian interpretation of the Tome failed to unite the Church. *The Arbiter* was immediately criticized on all fronts and John's cool analysis had to be defended immediately in a rather bitter polemic against the divorce of hypostasis and nature. He insisted that the concrete reality of Christ had to be one composite nature whose sensible reality was particular and whose intelligibility was not an Aristotelian universal apprehended by the mind, but a unique reality by virtue of its being centered in the divine logos or Word of God. He also attempted to insist that the Incarnation was a mystery about which no confusion of language should attempt to speak, a mystery that belonged to the glory of God's orders and structures in the world, against which is every and all sorts of evil. The Church's doctrines of Creation and Incarnation meant that the revelation of

God is to be apprehended in such a way that man becomes known as reconciled from his alienation and enmity towards the One Triune God who will not be known in any other way. Chadwick does not think Philoponos believed in three gods or intended anything less than the full humanity and deity of the God-Man. The Anathema of AD 680 is probably more an issue of the relation of reason and revelation and *The Arbiter* should be considered a theological work in response to very particular circumstances, and appreciated accordingly.[93]

Finally, Henry Blumenthal portrayed Philoponos as a Neoplatonist whose students, Elias for example, were capable of defending the eternity of primal matter and discussing the supersensual One of Plotinus, Proclus, and Ammonius. Ammonius, probably under imperial pressure and the Episcopate of Alexandria, agreed to allow Christian students to participate in the Academy and the debates over the eternity of the world. Dr. Blumenthal thinks Philoponos was a faithful student of Ammonius and probably the school's scribe. He concluded that his Christianity was of small moment in the Commentaries. Any good Neoplatonist could have held similar views to the Alexandrian Grammarian.[94]

Since the conference, Sorabji has published *Time, Creation and the Continuum*, in which is included an extensive discussion of the infinity arguments of Philoponos against Proclus and the debates over the eternity of the world. Sorabji agrees with Walzer that Philoponos got the best of the ancient pagans and in so doing provided the basis for the thought of Bonaventure, which Kant can only faintly echo in his *Critique of Pure Reason*.[95] But he has reservations about anyone's ability to prove the universe must have a beginning and does not think the arguments of Philoponos are absolutely compelling.[96] However, so far as the significance of Philoponos is concerned, he believes that the Grammarian deserves far more credit than scholars have given to him and must be thought of as a turning point in the history of philosophy. The problem may remain with us as concerns what we mean by <u>creatio ex nihilo</u>, and ambiguities may still be asserted about the intentions of Plato and Aristotle, but these problems do not militate against our need to bring the full range of the works of Philoponos into the English language. Sorabji promises to see this need met in fact, and already has planned that the translation of the *De opficio mundi* will be ready for publication very soon.[97] Stanley Jaki's remarks on Philoponos everywhere echo the value of Sorabji's concern. Of special concern should be, in my opinion, the way in which the concept of the contingency of the world allows the creative freedom and the appropriate framework by which real progress in science and theology might be made. It appears to me that this concept and its implications were not only at the heart of the way Philoponos was able, from within the great traditions of his time, to achieve that kind of harmony between empirical and theoretical aspects of the scientific method, in which human imagination and intuition, disciplined by the reality of the way things actually are, serve to help us grasp their real nature. Indeed, they provided the kind of concepts which allowed him to make real progress in physical theory. It also appears to me that those dichotomies which allow us to continue to analyze the world without being responsible to this kind of radical contingency are the real cause of the rationalistic and subjective tendencies in the race that allow us to become abstracted away from or pathetically existential about ourselves in the world. Of one such moment in the history of thought, Jaki has written:[98]

> The dichotomy will surprise no one moderately aware of the extent to which Christian thinkers can fall prey to the prevailing fashions of thought and of the extent to which they are prone to

fall back at all times on that most pagan of all ways of thinking, which prompts one consciously or subconsciously to eliminate the vista of contingency.

Most recently, Booth has attempted in fact to understand the thought of Philoponos as witnessing to a conversion to Aristotelian metaphysics.[99] It is argued that the Alexandrian scientist was interested in no more than preserving the Academy from closure as had happened at Athens. The accusation against him of Tritheism is a result of his embrace of Aristotelian ontology. He thereby ensured that Aristotle's influence was passed on to Arab and Syrian interests in cosmology and theology, through whom Western Christendom received the thought of the Grammarian. Booth suggests that St. Thomas Aquinas' synthesis of them is dependent upon John's radical Aristotelian ontology. He has repeated this claim with the publication of his book on this ontology and Christian thought.[100] It was this that led John to identify nature with hypostasis or individual reality. This was also responsible for the Monophysicism which led him inevitably to his Tritheism.[101] Philoponos is thus portrayed as a courteous controversialist about whom was experienced a revival of Aristotelian thought.[102] There is no attempt to discuss the revolutionary character of his thought, the Church's doctrine of creation out of nothing, and the contingency of the world and the way that these concepts, rooted in God's revelation of Himself, provided the foundation from which he built his physical theories even against the time honored convictions of the physics of the Ptolemaic Cosmology.

In the light of this tendency, in the light of the centuries of his obscurity, in the light of his condemnation, perhaps it is fitting to conclude this chapter with a catena of references which would attempt to reverse these judgments of his works:

The incorporation of these ideas in St. Basil's *Hexaemeron* played a very important role, not only in challenging the intellectual foundations of the classical outlook upon the world of visible and invisible reality, but in helping to transform the Greek mind in a way that has left its mark upon the very basis of our Western culture. Evidence for its far-reaching effect can be seen already in the fourth century in the *Hexaemeron* of St. Ambrose of Milan, and especially in the *De Opificio Mundi* of John Philoponos, the first great Christian physicist, in sixth century Alexandria.[103]

In the East the outstanding thinker concerned with light was John Philoponos of Alexandria. Working from a solid base in the teaching of Athanasius, Basil, and Cyril of Alexandria, he drew out the implications of the theological distinction between uncreated and created reality for the understanding of the contingent nature of the universe and its unitary rational order, thereby undermining and discarding the epistemological dualisms of Neoplatonists and Aristotelians alike.[104]

The bearing of that way of thinking (the onto-relational conceptualizations of classical Greek Patristic theology) is very evident in the formidable thought of John Philoponos of Alexandria, who, in the sixth century, worked out its implications for a reconstruction of ancient science and cosmology, in the course of which he developed a physics of light, a "modern" theory of impetus, and replaced the old receptacle notions of space and time with a thoroughly relational account of them, in astonishing anticipation of the twentieth century.[105]

For John Philoponos, however, who did not think in an Aristotelian way, in line with the theological and scientific tradition to which he belonged, nature meant "reality," so that for him to think of Christ as "one nature" meant that he was "one reality," and not a schizoid being. John Philoponos was no Monophysite in the heretical sense, but the accusation of heresy had the effect of denigrating also his anti-dualist thought in science and philosophy.[106]

Aquinas, as a child of his time, knew, for instance, of Philoponus only as one suspect of monophysitism and not as the seminal critic of Aristotle's cosmology and physics.[107]

John Philoponos was a thinker of epoch-making importance in the sixth century who taught philosophy in Alexandria in succession to Ammonius the son of Hermias, but who undertook a comprehensive and massive attack upon the foundations of Greek philosophy, science and religion from a distinctly Christian position.[108]

Philoponus' significance lies in his being, at the close of antiquity, the first to undertake a comprehensive and massive attack on the main tenets of Aristotle's physics and cosmology, an attack which was not repeated in thoroughness until Galileo.[109]

117

It seems evident that the sooner we can have access to the English translations of the works, the better we shall be able to appreciate the sharp contrast between scholars over their content and their significance in our modern world for both theology and science.[110]

NOTES TO CHAPTER THREE

1. R. Sorabji, "Infinity and the Creation: A Turning Point in the History of Philosophy," Inaugural Lecture, King's College, London University, March 16, 1982. Cf. *Time, Creation and the Continuum*, Cornell University Press, Ithaca, New York, 1983, pp. 197-98.

2. I. P. Sheldon-Williams, "The Greek Christian Platonist Tradition," in *The Cambridge History*, op. cit., pp. 425-531. He writes (p. 477): "Justinian's act was the gesture of a Christian prince silencing the enemies of the faith; but the enemies were not Platonism or even Neoplatonism, but the Procline theology based upon polytheism, and the Procline theurgy deriving from the belief in a supernatural power inherent in the phenomenal world."

3. Ibid., p. 483. Stephanus, a pupil of Philoponos, taught Grammar, Rhetorics, Dialectic, Arithmetic, Music, Geometry, and Astronomy in AD 610 in New Rome. The university tradition in the ancient world sought to educate students in the wisdom of "all" knowledge related to civic and family life, cf. A. Baumstark, *Syrisch Arabische Biographieren des Aristoteles*, Leipzig, Teubner, 1900, pp. 156-223.

4. E. A. Parsons, *The Alexandrian Library*, Cleaver-Hume Press, London, 1952.

5. H. I. Bell, "Alexandria," JEA XIII (1927), pp. 171- 84.

6. J. A. Thompson, "Alexandria," in ISBE, vol. I (1979), pp. 89-94. Strabo the Geographer is quoted on p. 91.

7. H. I. Bell, "Alexandria," JEA XIII (1927), pp. 171- 84. The author, against the thrust of the life of John Philoponos, sees Christian orthodoxy as against the "divine philosophy" which was the inspiration of much that Alexandria was.

8. E. A. E. Reymond and J. W. B. Barns, "Alexandria and Memphis: some historical observations," Orientalia, 46 (1977), pp. 1-33. The authors point out the struggle between the centers.

9. B. Farrington, *Science in Antiquity*, Oxford University Press, London, 1964, p. 98. Again, the author, against the significance of Philoponos' work, in the light of biblicists like Cosmas Indicopleustes (Sailor to India), who tried to prove from the Bible that the earth was flat, claims that Christianity did not encourage the discovery of truth in physical science.

10. B. Lovell, *Emerging Cosmology*, Columbia University Press, New York, 1981. See pp. 19-31 for the manner in which phenomenological data allows the false derivation of the rationality of the world.

11. Ibid., pp. 124-25.

12. Farrington, op.cit., p. 133.

13. H. I. Bell, op. cit., p. 178.

14. G. Boas, *Rationalism in Greek Philosophy*, John Hopkins Press,

Baltimore, 1961.

15. For example, cf. S. Sambursky and S. Pines, *The Concept of Time in Late Neoplatonism,* The Israel Academy of Sciences and Humanities, Jerusalem, 1971, pp. 9-21. I consider this problem the knot we need to untie in our time.

16. The *de Aeternitate Mundi contra Proclum* by John Philoponos was written explicitly against Proclus (AD 411- 485) and his arguments against Christian doctrines, especially the doctrine of creatio ex nihilo.

17. S. L. Jaki, *The Road of Science and the Ways to God,* University of Chicago Press, Chicago, 1978, pp. 19-33.

18. Ibid., p. 33.

19. Beside the above work by Jaki, see for example *Science and Creation,* Science History Publications, New York, 1974; *The Origin of Science and the Science of its Origin,* Regnery Gateway, South Bend, Indiana, 1978; and *Cosmos and Creator,* Regnery Gateway, Chicago, Illinois, 1980. Throughout Jaki's work attempts to champion the concept of the contingency of the world as God's creation.

20. The explication of this claim is also forced upon us by the works of Shmuel Sambursky. Cf. *Physics of the Stoics,* Macmillan, New York, 1959, and *The Physical World of Late Antiquity,* Basic Books, New York, 1962.

21. A. Einstein, et al., *The Principle of Relativity,* Dover Press, New York, 1952, papers first published in 1905, when the theory began to shape the legend the great scientist has become.

22. E. Wohwill, "Ein Vorgänger Galileis im 6. Jahrhundert," Phys-ikalischeZeitschrift, 7 (1906), pp. 23-32.

23. Ibid., p. 32.

24. G. Sarton, *Introduction to the History of Science,* vol. I, Williams & Wilkins, 1962 (1927).

25. Ibid., p. 422.

26. P. Duhem, *Le Système du Monde,* 10 volumes, Hermann, Paris, 1959.

27. Ibid., vol. I, pp. 313-321.

28. Ibid., vol. I, pp. 324, 333, 339, 351-56, 361-71, 381-85, 387, 388.

29. Ibid., vol. IV, pp. 506-7.

30. Ibid., vol. V, p. 545; vol. VI, p. 365; vol. VIII, pp. 173-82; vol. X, p. 216.

31. Ibid., vol. I, p. 398.

32. R. Taton, ed., *History of Science*, trans. A. J. Pomerans, Basic Books, New York, 1963.

33. W. Böhm, *Johannes Philoponos*, Verlag Ferdinand Schöningh, München, 1967. The echo in his time that Philoponos could not obtain for his thought is definitely begun to be heard here.

34. Cf. A. Güdeman, op. cit., col. 1764 and S. Sambursky, "John Philoponus," op. cit., p. 156, for Caesarea as his birthplace with A. H. Armstrong, op. cit., p. 478 and G. Verbeke, *Jean Philopon*, Universitaires de Louvain, Louvain, 1966, p. x.

35. Against Frend's assertion that the "Philoponoi" were a "ginger group" of "... pious intellectuals, bent on sniffing out the remains of paganism" (*The Early Church*, op. cit., p. 203), I would prefer to think of them as those disciples of the Lord who were devoted to seeking with "the eye of the soul" the Truth as the Truth compels itself upon our sincerity (cf. the opening sentence of *The Arbiter*). Böhm passes on the idea that it is the voluminosity of his works that gave him his surname (op. cit., p. 28), claimed to be some 3,000 pages of closely printed Greek.

36. Cf. H. Blumenthal, "John Philoponos and Stephanus of Alexandria: Two Neoplatonic Christian Commentators on Aristotle?" in *Neoplatonism and Christian Thought*, ed. D. J. O'Meara, International Society of Neoplatonic Studies, Norfolk, Virginia, 1982, pp. 54-63, with G. Verbeke, "Some Later Neoplatonic Views on Divine Creation and the Eternity of the World," in the same book, pp. 45-53. The views affect the effort to date the works of Philoponos.

37. G. Verbeke, op. cit., pp. 47-50.

38. W. Wieland, *Die aristotelische Physik*, Vandenhoeck and Ruprecht, Göttingen, 1970, pp. 59, 99, 110, 315.

39. P. Joannou, "Le premier essai chrétien d'une philosophie systematique," SP V (1962), p. 508.

40. W. Böhm, op. cit., p. 19.

41. Ibid., p. 23.

42. Ibid., p. 30.

43. Ibid., p. 31.

44. Ibid., pp. 32-62, where his theory of light is understood to be the foundation of the kind of thinking he will attempt in *The Arbiter*. This will be discussed later in the chapter, when I consider Jean Christensen's dissertation on *Philoponus and Aristotle*, but the claims of the scientist are startling: "Denn die erste Quelle des Lichtes hat Gott in die Sonne hineingelegt."

45. Ibid., pp. 182-88, 262-64, 300-6. Böhm claims that all the scientific concepts developed by Philoponos were based upon his belief that "Gott die ganze Welt aus nichts erschaften hat (p. 301)."

46. Ibid., pp. 301-2. The ἕνωσις ὑποστατική of his thought is always

a complete nature inseparable from both form and matter and yet distinguishable.

47. Ibid., p. 386 since writing my dissertation Philoponos' theory of light has been investigated by Jean de Groat, *Aristotle and Philoponus on Light*, Garland Publishing, Inc.; New York & London, 1991. The incoporeal nature of light in its relationality to the structure of matter is the problem here.

48. Ibid., pp. 389-90.

49. Ibid., pp. 394-95. The theory of created and creative correspondence between transcendent and experienced dimensions of reality, I believe, was at the heart of the science of Philoponos.

50. Ibid., p. 406.

51. M. R. Cohen and I. E. Drabkin, *A Source Book in Greek Science*, McGraw-Hill, New York, 1948.

52. Ibid., p. 219.

53. Ibid., p. 223.

54. M. Clagett, *Greek Science in Antiquity*, Collier, New York, 1955, pp. 206-23.

55. Ibid., pp. 220-23. W. Wright, *A Short History of Syriac Literature*, Black, London, 1894, claimed *The Arbiter* (Diaitetes) was a regular part of the curriculum in these Syriac schools. A. Vööbus, "The Origin of the Monophysite Church in Syria and Mesopotamia," CH 42 (1973), pp. 17-26 (see footnote 104, p. 26), claims *The Arbiter* was dedicated to Jacob Burdana of Edessa, the great Bishop of Monophysite churches and friend of Theodora.

56. S. Sambursky, *The Physical World of Late Antiquity*, Basic Books, New York, 1962. See p. 158 for quote.

57. Ibid., p. 156.

58. Ibid., p. 166.

59. S. Sambursky, *Physics of the Stoics*, Macmillan, New York, 1959, pp. 168-69. W. Böhm thinks it significant that Sambursky can compare the strife between the ancient philosophers to the controversy between Newton and Leibniz (JP, op. cit., p. 25).

60. Ibid., pp. 159-62.

61. Sambursky, *The Physical World*, op. cit., pp. 6-7.

62. Ibid., pp. 16-20, 168-72.

63. Ibid., p. 43.

64. Ibid., p. 87.   I think it important to be able to appreciate the

<u>zusammengesetzste</u> of the Alexandrian in opposition to the logico-causal necessary relations in Aristotle's thought (cf. W. Böhm, <u>JP</u>, op. cit., p. 62).

65. Ibid., pp. 156-58.

66. Ibid., p. 157.

67. Ibid., p. 174.

68. J. Christensen, *Philoponus and Aristotle*, History of Science Department, Harvard University Ph.D. dissertation, 1980. Cf. *de Anima* II, 7, 330.24:

69. Ibid., p. 25. Cf. W. Böhm, <u>JP</u>, op. cit., pp. 182- 88.

70. Ibid., pp. 26-56.

71. Ibid., pp. 82-92. Cf. W. Böhm, <u>JP</u>, op. cit., pp. 31-33.

72. S. Sambursky, "Philoponus' interpretation of Aristotle's theory of light," <u>Osiris</u> 13 (1958), pp. 114-26.

73. Ibid., pp. 123-26. Cf. T. F. Torrance, *Christian Theology and Scientific Culture*, op. cit., pp. 86-7.

74. R. B. Todd, "Some Concepts in Physical Theory in John Philoponus' Aristotelian Commentaries," <u>Archiv für Begriffsgeschichte</u> 24 (1980), pp. 151-70.

75. Ibid., pp. 151-52. The debate over the dating of the works and the influence of Christianity upon them is not settled. The complete works are listed in Güdeman's article and I would suggest we reserve our judgments until all of them have been considered, both scientific and theological.

76. Ibid., p. 155.

77. Ibid., p. 159. I believe this gave a dimension of depth and dynamical character to the Grammarian's theory of the universe which is necessary for true scientific culture. The modern debate between the Vatican and Stephan Hawking possesses many of the same problems

78. Ibid., p. 163.

79. Ibid., pp. 163, 168-70. Cf. M. Meyerhof, "Joannes Grammatikos (Philoponos) von Alexandrien und die arabische Medizin," *Mitteilungen des Deutschen Instituts für ägyptische Altertumskunde in Kairo* II (1932), pp. 1-21, where the Grammarian's reputation in medical theory has caused speculation about his being a doctor of medicine.

80. R. Walzer, "Greek into Arabic: Essay on Islamic Philosophy," <u>Oriental Studies</u>, eds. S. M. Stern and R. Walzer, vol. I, Cassirer, Oxford, 1962.

81. Ibid., p. 101.

82. Ibid., p. 191.

83. Ibid., p. 192.

84. Ibid., p. 193.

85. Ibid., p. 195.

86. Ibid., pp. 201-11.

87. Cf. H. A. Davidson, "John Philoponos as a source of mediaeval Islamic and Jewish proofs of creation," JAOS 89 (1969), pp. 357-91.

88. The conference is reported by T. F. Torrance, "John Philoponos of Alexandria: Sixth Century Christian Physicist", Texts and Studies, vol. II (1983), pp. 261-65. Since the writing of my dissertation, Sorabji has published the results of this conference in *Philoponus and the rejection of Aristotelian Science* (Cornell University Press: Ithaca, New York, 1987). The relationality of time and space to eternity remains the problem.

89. S. Sambursky, "Note on John Philoponus' Rejection of the Infinite," in *Islamic Philosophy and the Classical Tradition*, University of South Carolina Press, Columbia, S.C., 1972, pp. 351-53.

90. D. Furley, "Summary of Philoponus' Corollaries on Place and Void," to be published. Conference on Philoponus, June 2-4, 1983.

91. M. Wolff, *Geschichte der Impetustheorie*, Suhrkamp Verlag, 1978, and *Fallgesetz und Massbegriff*, DeGruyter, Berlin, 1971.

92. P. Hoffman, "Simplicius against Philoponus on the Nature of the Heavens," to be published. Conference on Philoponus, 1983. The translation is of Simplicius, *In de caelo*, 90, 11-21.

93. H. Chadwick, "Philoponus' Christian Theology," Conference on Philoponus, 1983, now published by Sorabji.

94. H. Blumenthal, "Philoponus, the Alexandrian Platonist," to be published, Conference on Philoponus, 1983. Cf. "John Philoponus and Stephanus of Alexandria: Two Neoplatonic Christian Commentators on Aristotle?" op. cit.

95. R. Sorabji, *Time, Creation and the Continuum*, Cornell University Press, New York, 1983, pp. 197-203.

96. Ibid., p. 224.

97. Richard Sorabji's collection of essays based upon the Philoponos conference: *Philoponos and the rejection of Aristotelian Science*, op. cit. now represents the most complete view of the Alexandrian scientists in English. Henry Chadwick's article (pp. 41-56) is a fine summary of the Grammarian's Christian writing. This is the best starting point for anyone interested in a survey of Philoponos' thought, but my reader will discern I am much more positive towards his contribution than appears in these articles. Christian Wildberg has also, since my writing produced an analysis of the 'Aether' according to the science of Philoponos (*John Philoponus' Critism of Aristotle's Theory of Aether*, (W. de Gruyter: Berlin and New York, 1988). It seems to

me that there is room for open structured thought at this point in our own time.

98. S. L. Jaki, *Cosmos and Creator*, op. cit., p. 128.

99. E. G. T. Booth, "John Philoponos: Christian and Aristotelian Conversion," <u>SP</u>, vol. I, Pergamon Press, New York, 1982, pp. 407-11.

100. Booth, *Aristotelian Aporetic Ontology in Islamic and Christian Thinkers,* Cambridge University Press, Cambridge, 1983, pp. 56-61.

101. Ibid., p. 59. Here he is in agreement with the assessment of Hermann's study.

102. Ibid., p. 61.

103. T. F. Torrance, *The Christian Frame of Mind*, The Handsel Press, Edinburgh, 1985, pp. 7-8.

104. _____, *Christian Theology and Scientific Culture*, Christian Journals, Belfast, 1980, p. 86.

105. _____, *Theology in Reconciliation*, Eerdmans, Grand Rapids, 1975, p. 12.

106. _____, *The Ground and Grammar of Theology*, University Press of Virginia, Charlottesville, 1980, p. 61.

107. S. L. Jaki, *The Road of Science and the Ways to God*, The University of Chicago Press, Chicago, 1980, p. 39.

108. T. F. Torrance, "John Philoponos of Alexandria, Sixth Century Christian Physicist," op. cit., p. 261.

109. S. Sambursky, "John Philoponos," in *The Encyclopedia of Philosophy*, vol. 6, Macmillan, New York, 1967, p. 156.

110. Cf. Nebelsick, H. P., *Circles of God,* Scottish Academic Press, Edinburgh, 1987. This provides us with an excellent example of the way the impact of Philoponos' thought has become to be appreciated.

CHAPTER FOUR

THE LIFE SETTING OF THE ARBITER
AND A LETTER TO JUSTINIAN

The Arbiter by John Philoponos, the Alexandrian Grammarian, was
probably commissioned by imperial appointment to provide a Christological
statement which the Holy Fathers of the Church might employ to achieve a
definition of the faith over which both Chalcedonians and Monophysites could
agree at the Fifth Ecumenical Council summoned by the Emperor Justinian to
Constantinople in AD 553. History has recorded its failure to accomplish this
purpose, and we have seen that its author had to defend its assertions in the
face of fervent criticism against him soon after the Council.[1] *The Arbiter* evidently is conceived as a dialogue consisting of ten chapters in which the union
of the divine and human natures of the person of Jesus Christ is explicated
with a view to defend the tradition of the theology of Cyril of Alexandria
against the condemned views of Nestorius and Eutyches ($\mu\acute{\iota}\alpha$ $\phi\acute{\upsilon}\sigma\iota\varsigma$ $\tau o\hat{\upsilon}$ $\Theta\epsilon o\hat{\upsilon}$
$\lambda\acute{o}\gamma o\upsilon$ $\sigma\epsilon\sigma\alpha\rho\kappa\omega\mu\acute{\epsilon}\nu\eta$). A review of the chapters has been offered by Hermann,
in which we are asked to understand that the scientist had taken seriously his
role as an umpire in a century-old debate.[2] He prefers to conceive of the
composition that is the reality of the union as one of two natures, so that the
unity is neither two things nor a new third thing. It is neither something that
is the result of joining or juxtaposition, but an individual reality in itself
which may not be defined as the common or universal nature of a species.
Neither is it a compound nature in two parts. It is a limited created nature in
a hypostatic reality manifestly one person, but that nature is a compound nature which exists and subsists only of the individual nature of the hypostasis
or person of the Word of God, which does not exist and subsist in numbered
parts. The best analogy for it is to be found in the world as that of the body

127

and soul relation with mankind. Each nature subsists in the individual so that there is in fact only one man, whose nature belongs to him and no other, and yet shares in the nature of the species as such. The differences of the natures, the one of the body and the one of the soul, may be contemplated as possessing the particular properties of their beings, but they in fact exist and subsist as one man, body of soul and soul of body in such a way that you cannot destroy the one without destroying the other. On the one hand we understand mankind in theory and on the other we experience Him only as the particular cases represented by Peter and Paul, etc. In light of these considerations, it is best, affirms Philoponos, to confess that Christ is "of" the Godhead and man and not "in" them.[3]

Again, history has recorded the failure of the effort. Severus' separated communion remained adamant against the Tome of Leo, and Philoponos, obviously still on friendly terms with Justinian, refused to journey to Constantinople to visit the Emperor because of his old age. The argument could not be explained personally by the Alexandrian Scientist to the Throne, and no advocate of Chalcedon, even those who had Justinian's desire for the unity of the Church of Jesus Christ throughout the Empire, so far as I can tell, ever found it compelling. *The Arbiter* was attacked by members of both parties, and when Philoponos died, sometime about AD 575, one gets the impression that he was surrounded by adversaries on every front, scientific and theological. About one hundred years later, he had become associated in the West with the condemned Severus, and officially, as we have seen, anathematized in AD 680 by the Sixth Ecumenical Council as a Monophysite. The Monophysites in the East had already condemned him as a Tritheist. We have also seen how his struggle against the addiction of the Greek mind to the concept of an eternal cosmos, where the immutability and the impassibility of the divine held out to an immortal soul a light up which one might climb out of the mu-table and temporary nature of earthly things, was also an historical failure. As a scientist, he had to see the contingent, free, and unique reality of the creation of God turned by his contemporaries into the static thing that would control the thought of Byzantium and the West alike for centuries to come, the effort of such Fathers of the Church as Athanasius, Basil, and Cyril swamped by efforts to build with one logical bridge after another a way across the chasm that separated man from the divine.[4] The free and creative way that God Himself had taken with the dynamical world of His creation, where His mystery and reality is made known with a love and grace that would help us to understand why we had been made to be, became a truth that was the enemy of one synthesis after another between the cosmology of the world and the theology of the Creator. I believe I see still today that the uniqueness, freedom, and contingency of our world remains greatly unappreciated, and it seems to me we would do well to become better acquainted with the works of one of our fathers in the faith who, when he denied any self-explaining logos to the universe, desired to point others to that Word of God which he had heard in Christ, the incarnate Savior whose death and resurrection in the world meant for all those who believe the gift of an immortal life whose light would forever be the very light of God Himself with us, Jesus Christ our Lord. In this sense, history's failure can hardly mean for us anything more than a temporary delay of a true appreciation of the Alexandrian scientist.

I would like to conclude my study of the life-setting of *The Arbiter* by John Philoponos with an offering of a translation of the letter he wrote his king, the Emperor Justinian, defending one last time that for which he had tried to argue in response to his imperial appointment. I do not expect that it will itself cause us any deeper insights into the problem of thinking through consistently the nature of the reality of the person of Jesus Christ. When we attempt to apprehend with our minds the truth of the Eternal Spirit, whose Triune Being is holy ground indeed, and to know the love of the Son of God with the love of the Father, we must with the fathers of the Church listen with our hands clapped over our mouths, lest we should replace with our own words the very Word of God Himself to our kind. The problem of explicating the rationality of the being, nature, hypostasis, and person of this Word must be done then in such a manner that the divine orders implied are never lost from our arguments, and we can by the grace of God really make every effort in our freedom to worship Him together in Spirit and in truth. Would this not provide the real ground upon which we might break through to those in our own time who know only the silence of God in the terrible beauty of the nature of the world? In any case, the centuries of debate between Chalcedonians and Monophysites in the One Holy Catholic and Apostolic Church of Jesus Christ will not be resolved without appreciating, I believe, the struggle of Philoponos and His Emperor.

A Letter to the Emperor Justinian[5]

"Again, the same, John Philoponos: a letter to the Emperor Justinian.

1.   When Stephanos, the trustworthy servant of Your God-fearing Majesty, informed me, O Philanthropic Emperor, that Your Serene Highness had commanded to bring my lowly self to the God-fearing feet of the Universal Lord over all of us, next to God, and that I was to be esteemed worthy of the Your Sight and to pay homage to your Philanthropy, your God-loving Piety which is towards all mankind, which is most fitting for royalty that imitates God, this strengthened my soul, that I might hasten to possess all of this beneficence, and yet old age and great infirmity of body has necessarily made me very reluctant to travel, indeed it is impossible to undertake the labor of any journeys with weaknesses such as these, especially in the time of winter. However, Stephan, the servant of Your Philanthropic Majesty, insisted, indeed he was even adamant, that I should send at least some kind of petition on behalf of the universal peace of Mankind. Yet this seemed to me an even more fearsome command than the former, that I should dare to speak on parchment and in ink to the One who has been entrusted by Our Lord Christ with the reins of all the world. But when I considered that we are commanded to speak at all times by means of prayers and petitions even to God, the Maker of All, I thought, 'Why should this be a shameful thing?' Surely, it is all the more necessary rather than shameful that we should send petitions to the Great Emperor who in his benevolence towards humanity is compared even to God, we who are at all times dependent upon your Serene Highness.[6]

2.   So all these considerations have persuaded me to venture to write,

especially since I know that purpose of Your Serene Majesty would urge to unite all those who desire to worship God because of the incarnation of the great God, even Our Savior Jesus Christ, who guards your life on account of the purity of your faith that is in Him. For who, among those kings of antiquity which had received the mystery of Christ, has proclaimed so clearly the Worship of the True Religion, which is in Him, such as Your Christ-Loving Majesty, who every day teaches:[7]

(This is a formal credal statement)

> The Son of God and the Word,
> the Maker of all things (Pantokrator),
> who is from everlasting God with God the Father,
> Who begat Him who is above the ages
> and through whom God even the Father has made the ages,
> the same who in these latter days has become a man,
> when He was incarnated by the Holy Spirit
> and by the Theotokos,[8] the ever-virgin Mary,
> whose flesh is consubstantial with us,[9]
> and possesses a rational and intelligent soul,
> which is also consubstantial with our own soul,
> while His divinity is not changed into flesh,
> and His holy flesh is not changed into divinity,[10]
> the same who was crucified in the flesh,
> Our Lord Jesus Christ,
> who willingly tasted death on our behalf
> and who rose from the dead after three days
> and ascended into heaven.
> He is one of the blessed and consubstantial Trinity.[11]

Moreover, who else mocks the Man-Worship of the impious Nestorius in words and deeds like Your Invincible Majesty, who has, if I may speak bluntly, repudiates all heresies? Because of these things, God has crowned Your Divine Head with victory over all the Barbarians.[12] For, indeed, 'those who glorify me I will glorify,'[13] and He reserves great honor, conferring upon them after this one here the very same Kingdom of Heaven (where God dwells). For I say that the unity of the Holy Church of God, which adheres to Your Doctrines, and which I have affirmed above, may be achieved through

Your very own diligence, after God, O God-fearing Lord, if you will esteem worthy of correction this argument containing the present danger. For it is a superfluous claim not in accord with your own orthodox and God-pleasing thought and has divided the Church of God up until this very day, which will never be united unless it is by proclamation outlawed.[14] As to the fact that it affirms that there are two natures to Christ in conflict with the orthodox thinking and doctrines of Your Majesty, which have just now been set forth (i.e. the Credo above), we will now briefly explain.

3.   How can the unity of the divine nature and of the human one from which Our Lord Jesus Christ has been completed, be properly thought and confessed concerning Him if these things which have been united did not become one thing in reality? Now it is evident that this occurs without change and without confusion, each one of these remaining as its own nature without ending up merged into the other,[15] just as also a man, who is of a soul and a body, is one nature, while the incorporeal soul is not changed into a body and the body is not changed into the incorporeal being (ousia) of a soul.[16] For if his unity exists merely in relations of honor or only an association of persons, such as Nestorius prefers, without the natures with their hypostasis being united, as Your God-fearing Majesty teaches, then it must be absolutely necessary that Christ, who has been composed of them, must be composed as one nature.[17] For if, as honors and persons these are joined according to Nestorius, and not as natures and hypostases, but as Nestorius has said, there is one honor and one person to the two natures that were there, how is it not necessary that those who confess a hypostatic union of these natures, should also confess that there exists a single nature and hypostasis, to him who has been united from the two? But how can these two things, which have been united in a composition, be explained if the one thing from which the

composition has been completed ceases to exist? For the fact is that the union is named as one thing, just as whiteness is from white![18] For in the same way that something which has been made white is white as it participates in whiteness and a body which has assumed life is alive, so the thing which has been made one thing out of something, in that it participates in the union, by all means has become one thing.[19] And contrariwise, if one thing is divided, and therefore no longer exists as a particular thing, because of the division, then it has become two things. For how is it possible, when the natures have not been united, that they could also exist as two in the one thing they constitute, whatever it is that they have become, except that they should remain two (natures) while they have been united? For in this way, they will have remained divided. For what is more clear than these things, or rather assured to those who do not seek to argue vainly, than the fact that it is not right to devise these things about God and the Truth for those who fear God, who sees into the depths of our thought?

4.   Already for some time now, Your God-Fearing Majesty has very wisely conceived and taught that Our Lord Christ is one composed hypostasis, as, indeed, I also confess that Christ is composed.[20] If, therefore, that one thing which is composed is the one hypostasis of Christ, which is the same as saying that Christ is composed of different natures or hypostases, that is without change, then it is absolutely necessary that the nature of Christ is also composed as one thing, since the nature of each and every single thing is the same as the hypostasis, as even the Teachers (of the Church) have also affirmed.[21] Consequently, one understands the following: The Holy and Blessed Trinity is proclaimed and confessed by us as an equality in ousia, possessing, indeed, divine efficacies and clear demonstrations. However, being equal in ousia does not mean an existence as something in and of itself;

being equal in ousia by all means is existence as one thing in another thing or other things, just as Peter and Paul and the rest of the race are equal in ousia with one another. For that definition which Paul receives as a man, rational mortal animal, is received by every man.[22] In the same way, every single one of the hypostases of the Holy Trinity, is equal in ousia with the other two that remain. For whatever the being (ousia) of God is, the same is the Father and the Son and the Holy Spirit, so that God is every single one of them. Hence, it is evident, then, that every single one of the hypostases is not some other thing outside of that nature which is in every single one of them.[23] This can be looked at in another way also: Your Divine Majesty also confesses 'the one nature of God the Word become incarnate' with the Holy Fathers,[24] and he teaches the True Religion. For not all of the Holy Trinity has become incarnate, but only the Son of God and the Word. For when we affirm the fact that the one nature of the Trinity, that of the Word become incarnate, this is that then which defines the Word God.[25] Indeed, while confessing that the nature of the Father is distinguished from that of the Spirit, it is clear that each and every one of the three hypostases also signifies a nature. And when, therefore, this is thus clearly perceived, as I suppose is the case now for everyone, then if one affirms the one composed hypostasis of our Lord Christ, it is also necessary that we confess he is himself one composed nature. For it has been seen that the nature of each single thing is also the same as the hypostasis. So if we affirm that Christ is two natures, then it is necessary by all means that we should speak of his two hypostases, a doctrine which has its source in Paul of Samosata, a blasphemy inherited by Nestorius the uprooter of Your Majesty.[26]

5.   But how it is possible, they ask, that the one nature can be both the nature of the Godhead and that of the humanity? I agree that the whole thing

135

is utterly impossible for the one who doubts! But is it not that the essential hypostasis of God and Man should become one thing among those things that are possible?[27] For if the one hypostasis of Christ is composite thing, as, indeed, Your God-fearing Majesty rightly teaches, how may this hypostasis of a simple Godhead exist as that which is not simple but composite? Therefore, just as the hypostasis of which Christ, which is composed, is not an individual hypostasis of his divinity, by itself, nor again the hypostasis of his ensouled flesh, by itself, but belongs to him who has been composed of the two of them, namely Our Lord Jesus Christ, so too the composed nature of his Godhead does not exist by itself, nor further His Humanity by itself, but belongs to the Christ who is that one which has been composed of the two of them, seeing that it has been shown that it (the nature) and the hypostasis are the same.[28] Why, therefore, should we fear to confess his nature as one composite nature, when we feel confident about confessing that our Lord Jesus Christ is one composite hypostasis? For whether one speaks of hypostasis or nature of Christ, he does not refer to anyone other than Christ the Lord. But what further objection do they bring forth? They say, indeed, the hypostasis of Christ is one thing, since his ensouled flesh did not previously exist before the union with the Word, when he assumed existence. What then follows? Did the nature of the flesh, which was united with the Word, previously exist before its union with him, so that they can claim that Christ possesses two natures? But this is blasphemy as well as absurd! Indeed, this is just what the impious Paul of Samosata and Nestorius liked to think! For because they posit that a nature existed without an hypostasis before the union, this is the same as someone saying that he existed before the union and that he does not exist.[29] But, indeed, we say there are two natures of Christ, the universal divinity and the universal humanity.'[30] But we have already said, more than often enough, that the universal nature of humanity and the universal (nature) of divinity did not become the union, but that nature alone of God, the Word, joined with the nature of the ensouled flesh alone, which was assumed with the Theotokos. And this, indeed, Your Serene Highness rightly has taught--that whatever is without a limit is also without a hypostasis. For of such kind is that which is termed a universal, and, indeed, it is clear that it is not possible for such a thing to be composed.[31] For how can that which does not possess it own existence by itself be conceived, except in <u>theoria</u>?[32] So only the nature of the ensouled flesh which was assumed with the Theotokos is united to the Word God, which did not previously exist before the union with Him. `For wisdom has built the house!'[33] If, therefore, these universals have not been united, it is not possible, then, for us to affirm that Christ possesses two universal natures. For then we would have to claim that these are two hypostases that existed without definition (limit). For just as the common Word exists as a nature, so also it exists as a hypostasis. So if these natures, which have become with one another the composition, are partials (opp. universals), from which the Christ exists, and because the nature did not previously exist before that flesh which was united with the Word, but was created in the Word, then we must affirm, indeed, the one nature of Christ, just as we affirm his hypostasis is one, or we would clearly be saying that there are two natures and two hypostases along with Nestorius. Therefore, when they assert so carelessly that Christ is, indeed, one hypostasis, without defining it as being composed, while they affirm he is two natures even after the union, and not only this, but they also anathematize indiscriminately those who would affirm the one nature of Christ, it is clear that they imagine in this manner they can deceive the two parties, those who on the one hand, teach the doctrines of Nestorius, by means of the phrase "of two natures", and those who, on the other hand, teach the doctrines of the Holy Fathers, with whom Your Piety concurs, by means of the phrase, "of one hypostasis", nevertheless they cannot conceal the fact that they have strayed from both of them.[34]

6.   But doubtless someone has said, while tacitly inclined towards the True Religion: To speak of two natures of Christ is very clearly the position of those dividing (Him), whereas with the phrase "in two natures" this is no longer the case, since the ancients customarily spoke about the universal in the parts. But whoever says this does not know that the ancients would affirm that the universal exists in the parts of those things only whose parts exist in the same space with one another, so that they are not separated from the universal, those of a human being are likewise called parts, the flesh and the bones and the nerves and such things as these, and those organs from which come the head, the arms, the feet, and those that belong to the innards, the liver, the heart, the kidneys, and the rest of the organs such as these. Now concerning these things that are not separated from one another in space, from which exists a composition, where all of them permeates through all of them, like the soul and the body (for by means of all of the body the soul exists), no one has ever said about them, who knows how to speak with precise arguments, that a human being exists in a soul or in a body, but of a soul and of a body.[35] And concerning the four elements,[36] of which the body is composed, no one among the Sages attempted to demonstrate that the flesh or the bones exist in four elements, but of the four elements, and fire and water are not in matter and form but of matter and form. For all of it in all of it exists three- dimensionally,[37] that is as three extensions, a form resulting distinctively with the other two. In the same way, we think of those things which have been crafted together: The house, on the other hand, is said

to be exist in the stones and in the wood beams and in such things as these, or in the walls and in roofs and in doors and such things as these, for considered in their places these can be distinguished from one another. But a bronze statue, say of a human being, exists of bronze and of a human form, and does not exist in these things. For the shape resembling some man does not exist separately in space from the bronze. And everything is conceived in this manner. Consequently, on the one hand, concerning those parts which are separated in the whole and of which it is correct to say--as, indeed, I do say--`The house is composed of stones and wood beams and in these things, as I have said, because the universal (whole) does exist in parts that are separate from one another. But, on the other hand, concerning those things which are not thus divided, but subsist by means of the universal, these things are only ever said to be of these and never in these things. If, then, the divinity of our Lord Christ permeates entirely His holy flesh, just as the rational soul permeates all of the body, and does not exist merely in any particular part, by itself, as the head and the arms are in a man, then it is not possible to affirm that Christ exists in two natures, as a universal exists in parts, but rather the divinity and the humanity exists of two natures. So much for the dispute mentioned above! Those who have posited, then, that Christ has two natures and exists in two natures, while taking these as indicators by analogies, are clearly introducing, by the use of each of them, a separation of the natures, just as one might speak of the person of the Emperor as appearing in all of his officials, and thereby they make it evident that they have eschewed the phrase "of two natures" as that signification which denotes the composition. Consequently, for Nestorius and those who have been trained by him, it is customary and desirable to affirm the phrase `in two natures,' while they absolutely reject (the phrase) "of two." But, as I have already indicated, the one signifies a composition, the other a division. Therefore, I understand that those who affirm that Christ has two natures <u>in</u> two natures are introducing through each one of them a separation of the natures. Hence, each one of these phrases that oppose Your God-fearing ideas on Christ's behalf and the doctrines of the Fathers should absolutely be avoided. For the testimonies of the Doctors of the Holy Church, which agree with these things, You, the Universal Lord of everyone, you know very well, and more than often enough, so to speak, you have expounded them to everyone, so that to quote them any further would be superfluous.[38]

7.   I have written these few things which I have gathered from so many of the teaching of Your Majesty and the Holy Fathers, so that we might expound from them the True Religion and the precise arguments by means of which we could explicate, as far as possible, our ideas to you, O my God-fearing Lord. Now to the Majesty alone of Your invincible Christ-loving Empire, O Serene Lord, may Christ the great God, before whom you fear, lovingly keep for you great honor and heavenly provisions for your journey to God, after a good old age, and may the language about the two natures, which has been the cause of so much stumbling and division to the Church of God, and concerning the phrase `in two,' which is less than suitable for the exposition of the division, alone with the advocates and the defenders of Nestorius, who hate Christ, be thrown out of the Church of Christ, so that we do not glory in any other thing than the grace which all the greatness of God has assumed. Now to the one who restores all the Preeminent Empire of the Romans, may God by all means grant by the Word of the Orthodox Confession, who from antiquity was endowed with the word of faith, the unity of the Church. The letter of John Philoponos to the God-loving Justinian, Emperor of the Romans, is concluded."

The letter is dated approximately AD 560, seven years after the Fifth Ecumenical Council and just a few years before the death of the Grammarian. I believe it indicates clearly that the heart of the problem between the parties must be considered to be the relation between nature and person, or hypostasis, and the prepositions "in" and "of" employed to explicate this relation can be meaningfully discussed only within a coherent grasp of both the cosmology and the theology of the scientist. The historical failure of the argument and the Fifth Ecumenical Council to compel any agreement in the East and the West is a fact whose consequences remain with us even today,[39] a mute testimony to the Church's inability or unwillingness to discover a rational ground for its worship upon which both West and East might conceive an expression of the Apostolic Faith which both could call home. But may this not be, after all, accredited to our failure to work out the real way in which the relation between the Doctrines of Creation and Incarnation must be explicated in a real world?

It seems to me that the concerns of John Philoponos to interpret Chalcedon and Constantinople II in a Cyrillian framework of thought, whose dynamics and structures are shaped and sustained by the creatio ex nihilo and the concept of the real contingency of the order and rationalities we discover with the world, are far from angels dancing upon the heads of perennial pins or abstract efforts to busy skeptical philosophers over our nothingness, but a passionate effort to serve for the best an Emperor who believed that, somehow, the nature of the world and the nature of God were ultimately and redeemingly bound up with the nature of Christ and salvation, Christ and His Gospel. I do not believe that we should allow the failures of history to shape our attitudes about the value of our efforts to apprehend the meaning of our lives in the vast and tremendous thing the universe is, to think that the Alexandrian Scientist was merely concerned with imposing upon the truth of

God and the world philosophical categories which would idealize the way things have actually been made to be and really are.

The life-setting of *The Arbiter* by John Philoponos must be conceived to be the very nature of space and time, of matter and energy, light and human life itself, the creation viewed in the light of the Word of the Savior and the Creator. It is evident that he was, as we are of ours, a child of his times, who had to struggle with the traditional and expected ways of understanding this setting, but who again and again demonstrated that it is possible to think afresh with such force that new ground is broken for a new understanding of the foundations of our knowledge. His struggle with the fundamentals of Aristotelian notions of eternity, infinity, space, time, and motion, and with the popularity of the Ptolemaic Cosmology, is proof enough of how tradition and the creative genius of the individual together can and will be the stuff out of which civilization is achieved. That his struggle could produce concepts which must themselves for centuries also struggle to win the minds and hearts of the race, that we can see him as a forerunner in science to the space and motion of Galileo and Newton's mechanics, that his theories of light and the role of the human imagination in the creating of a real correspondence between the theoretical and the empirical in our commitment to apprehend the reality of what we experience as mortal creatures, is telling enough about the value of his efforts. There is no doubt that the scientific community acts responsibly when it would make new efforts to appreciate the science of Philoponos. But it seems to me that it is more than evident that we cannot think these concepts were developed in isolation from his belief in the Lord God and the way that belief affected the fecundity of his thought about the nature of the world. To do this is to cause a split in his thinking where no such dichotomy ever existed, and to see him in some fragmented fashion in such a manner as to prevent a true appreciation of his work and thought within our

142

civilization. However difficult it is for us, we must be committed to appre-hending the real though contingent relations between God and the world, by that Word of God which was always at the center of Philoponos' thought. The Grammarian inherited both the scientific traditions developed in the Golden City and the great Episcopate tradition of Alexandria. To think together the One Triune God in Christ meant for Philoponos that a light had been given by the Creator in such a way that even the created light of the world could be understood by His power, on the contingent basis implicated with the freedom of the creation, by a creative correspondence to that which must be made real by Christ Himself. Here, thought Philoponos, was the proper ground for God's interaction with his world.[40] Upon this ground, ancient problems of the whole and the parts, the infinite and finite, could be explicated in such a way that both the nature of the world and the nature of God could be truly and ap-propriately apprehended.[41] And from this basis a dynamically relational way of thinking could be brought to light which was truly cogent for science and theology. The transcendence of God and the reality of God's interaction with the cosmos and the creature could be explicated, not in terms of logical par-adoxes and dialectical syntheses of thoughts abstracted from the reality of the Word of God in the world, but of open and dynamic orders of thought ca-pable of witnessing, with what they are made to be, to the love and mercy and forgiveness of the great God and Lord of the universe. I believe that this is the life-setting of *The Arbiter*, a world-view far more significant than any of the politics with which Justinian had to be concerned, and that it could pro-vide for us in our own time the means by which we might think afresh of the nature of our reconciliation with our Creator.

This means, I believe, a new translation and fresh interpretation of the argument of *The Arbiter* should be forthcoming. A real effort ought to be made to appreciate the argument in the light of the ground Philoponos broke in order to overcome the Ptolemaic cosmology and the Aristotelian Physics popular in his day. This, I believe, might allow us to give fresh definitions to the relations of nature, hypostasis, and person, and the way a preposition can make a difference in the expression of our intentions might be appreciated in such a manner as to allow a real reconciliation to be achieved in the love God is for the world. I think that it is possible, for instance, to consider the terms ousia, phusis, hypostasis, and prosopon as related in specific ways to a coherent field of reality through which their functions might be apprehended as whole and parts without confusing the one for the other. This would allow us to interpret their relationships, not in some linear correspondence, but in the dynamical character of the depths inherent in the hierarchy of truth itself, where invisible and visible dimensions of being are given truly appropriate definitions, and I believe would allow us not only to be more faithful to *The Arbiter* and its life-setting, but also to throw some light upon the division between East and West over the relation between nature and person in Christology. as well as upon the problems our science wrestles in our time.

There is a passage from Philoponos' *Contra Aristotelem*, which had been lost because Simplicius had ignored it in his argument with the *De caelo* of the Grammarian, and is now recovered by Arabic scholars. Perhaps I can best conclude my study with it, and allow Philoponos himself to have the last word:[42]

> Therefore, if many men believe that the divine cause dwells in heaven, it ought not to be thought that this is proof that they also believe [heaven] to be imperishable and ungenerated. Rather, they must believe that this place is more illumined by the light of God than another, just as they believe that one place is more appropriate for God than another, and just as it is thought that one man is closer or more remote from God than another according to the light of God shed upon him as a result of his good behavior and fine actions. For all things are filled with God, and it is impossible that anything at all be devoid God. And the light of God is shed upon everything according to its conduct during its life or according to its nature.

NOTES TO CHAPTER FOUR

1. W. Böhm, op. cit., p. 432.

2. Th. Hermann, op. cit., pp. 239-42. Hermann does not seem to grasp the way Philoponos conceives the relation between the universal and particular natures of a hypostatic reality or person. Although his analysis is thorough, he does not seem to appreciate how the Grammarian solved the problem of the whole and the parts without being confined to logico-causal and necessary relationships only. However, he does indicate that Philoponos attacked the law of non-contradiction when he considered the theological categories in the discussion (p. 231).

3. Ibid., p. 241, recalling, however, that the analysis is made within a non-Ptolemaic and non-Aristotelian view of the world.

4. Cf. G. Florovsky, "The Concept of Creation in Saint Athanasius," SP, vol. III, IV (1962), pp. 36-57.

5. A. Šanda, *Ioannis Philoponi, Opuscula Monophysitica*, op. cit., pp. 123-30. Cf. W. Böhm, *Johannes Philoponos*, op. cit., pp. 434-37. There is also a translation of the letter into Italian by G. Furlani, "Una lettera di Giovanni Filopono all'imperatore Guistiniano," AIVS 79:2 (1919-20), 1247-65, which I have not been able to obtain. I would like to thank especially Professors Geoffrey W. Bromiley and Frederick W. Bush of Fuller Theological Seminary and Sebastian Brock of The Oriental Institute at the University of Oxford for their gracious help in the translation of the letter. I could not have begun without my mentors from Fuller and without Professor Brock's gracious correction of my weaknesses I would have no confidence that I have understood. The Syriac translation of the original Greek does not make for easy reading, and there are many points of obscurity in relation to understanding the texts. Without attempting to put it into 'good' English, I have tried to render as clearly as possible the conceptual power of the Arbiter's thought.

6. In this highly formal address of Justinian, I see no cynical intention. Severus of Antioch had been exiled for more than a decade when the letter was written, which means Philoponos was not absolutely identified with him by the imperial power. His relationship with Justinian should help us make this distinction.

7. The basic adherence of the Alexandrian Scientist to the doctrinal decrees of Justinian are affirmed.

8. "yldt ʾlhʾ" was the title for Mary demanded in the East as the confession which guarded against any Nestorian interpretation of the natures of Christ. The cry of the Θεότοκος was the popular affirmation of the Christology of Cyril of Alexandria. Cf. W. H. S. Frend, *The Rise of the Monophysite Movement*, Cambridge University Press, Cambridge, 1972.

9. This is the confession of the homoousios championed by Athanasius at Nicea (d-swt ln b-ʾosyʾ) is literally "equal to us in being"). Cf. chapter 7 of *The Arbiter* for the way this confession is fundamental to the context in which the terms ousia, nature, hypostasis and person are to be understood.

10. Here Philoponos confesses his embrace of Chalcedon and the in-

tention of its four adverbs, where Christ is understood to be fully God and fully man, though without sin.

11. It was important for the Orthodox in the East to confess that Christ as a man was yet one of the Trinity. It is at the heart of the assertions of Cyrilline Christology, and resonates with the perception that his flesh subsists only in the hypostatic reality of the Word of God, and never in and of itself.

12. We have noted that Justinian had been able to restore the boundaries of the Empire established by Constantine. Persia, Africa, Italy, and Spain had all experienced the Emperor's might.

13. Cf. I Samuel 2:30b. Philoponos alludes to the man of God's prophecy to Eli, whose sons had turned their backs upon the laws of God, because of which Samuel was to be raised up in Israel.

14. I think he means the phrase "in two natures."

15. Again, Philoponos is confirming his acceptance of the intention of the four adverbs of Chalcedon.

16. I think it is important to recognize the way in which Philoponos understood the validity of the use of analogy. The correspondence is not a comparison of image, but real involvement if in a way we cannot image for ourselves.

17. It is important to notice here that natures (kyn³) and hypostases (qnôm³hon) are plural, becoming here a singular nature.

18. The point in the thought of John Philoponos is that the intelligible and the sensible, form and matter, the theoretical and the empirical may not be divorced from one another. Even if with imageless relation, that with which a thing participates is what the thing is, just as the ray of the sun and the sun are one.

19. This can then be understood as a primitive form of the concepts of anhypostasis and enhypostasis implicit in the Incarnation's signification. Cf. T. F. Torrance, *Theology in Reconstruction*, op. cit., pp. 130-49.

20. W. Böhm's translation is "zusammengesetzte Hypostase," and bears most vividly the idea that the reality of Christ is established as a particular man of a whole who is the Word of God.

21. Our study has made it clear that Philoponos must mean Athanasius, Basil, Cyril, and Severus. Cf. T. F. Torrance, "Athanasius: A Study in the Foundations of Classical Theology," in *Theology in Reconciliation*, op. cit., pp. 215-266 for this background to the μία φύσις to be confessed of the Son.

22. Ibid., p. 126. These are categories derived from the Porphyrian Tree common to the curriculum at the Academy of Alexandria. The reception of form was a common principle of the school, and the dynamics that a universal informed a species irreversibly is basic to Philoponos' argument.

23. It is important here that we do not identify nature, hypostasis,

and being (ousia) here in a linear relationship as Herman has done: ὑπόστασις, φύσις, ἄτομον, ὕπαρξις stehen auf einer Linie (p. 217). The "pleonastic" character of the thought, noted by Lebon, must be appreciated. Cf. Diogenes Allen, *Philosophy for Understanding Theology*, Atlanta, John Knox Press, 1985, chapter 4 for a good modern analysis of the way these categories of thought were developed to serve classical Greek theology. But the dynamical character of the thought of Philoponos must be appreciated with real between levels of reality differentiation.

24. This means, as has already been suggested, that Philoponos believes he is saying the same thing as Athanasius and Cyril of Alexandria.

25. Again, this is the doctrine of the anhypostasis of the flesh of Christ.

26. Paul of Samosata (265-270) seems to have defended a form of Adoptionism which was also condemned at both Nicea and Chalcedon. Philoponos claims a trajectory may be traced from him into the conflict between Cyril and Nestorius.

27. W. Böhm translates qnôm⁾ ⁾ôsy⁾ d-ᶜlh⁾ with "Seinhypostase Gottes," following A. Sanda's "hypostasis essentialis Dei." The point is, it seems to me, that no universal grounded in the Logos of God can be thought as one created reality among many created realities. He is in the first place uncreated.

28. The phrase ḥô d-ḏ-ḥôyô kd hô is considered to be in error by Šanda, who would write: hô d-hoyo kd ho. "Quam [naturam] eaudem et hypostasim esse probatum est." Böhm writes, "Womit auch bewiesen ist, dass Natur dasselbe ist wie Hypostase." I have taken it to justify his argument that, if the hypostasis has been composed, so must the nature of Christ.

29. Philoponos would accuse the Nestorian interpretation of the natures as a number rationality imposed unreally upon the actuality of the union. It is important to appreciate in the thought of the scientist the function time has in what things truly are.

30. I have sometimes translated (kolnyt⁾) "common" but it is the category of "universal" in the Porphyrian Tree which is being contemplated. Our tendency to abstract "universals" prevents me from using it always, for the thought of Philoponos would not posit a separation between universals and species, but a dynamic hierarchy of being, which may not be thought of as separate from a given essence or being. cf. I.R. Torrance, *Christology After Chalcedon*, St. Mary's Plain, Norwich, Norfolk: The Canterbury Press, 1988, where the opposite (dylyt⁾) is well investigated.

31. Limitation and definition is what the individual and particular species of a common genus receive, according to the categories belonging to the Prophyrian Tree employed at the Academy in Alexandria.

32. I have transliterated this word because it is just as crucial to the exposition as nature, hypostasis, being (ousia), and person. Cf. T. F. Torrance, "Truth and Authority in the Church," in *Transformation and Convergence in the Frame of Knowledge,* op. cit., pp. 310-12 for its discussion. If we apprehend the dynamical character of the thought of Philoponos, we will take this to mean that the universal category grasped by the intellect may

not be abstracted from a real integration with the individual categories belonging to the phenomenal world. We will not then be tempted to accuse John of nominalism, as I think is reflected in Böhm's translation of Sanda's Latin: "Denn wie soll denn das, was nicht einmal eine eigenständige Existenz hat, sondern nur im Denken des Verstandes effasst wird, wirklich zusammengesetzt werden können?" (op. cit., p. 436).

33. Proverbs 9:1. This means to assert a divine causality to which all the causality of the world can only be related through contingent correspondences where the freedom of the divine is fully respected.

34. This is a very cumbersome sentence, but I think it demonstrates how Philoponos intended to mediate a position to which both parties in the debate might agree, while continuing to protect the definition of the faith against Nestorian tendencies.

35. The concept is that "in" allows for number rationality which is related quantitatively to space, while "of" allows for a rationality which cannot be measured. Space, place, and matter or energy are conceived uniquely by Philoponos to be defined by the divine power ultimately.

36. I.e., formless matter (hôl²), formed species (dyš²), fire (nôd²) and water (my²). These were fundamental elements in the Ptolemaic Cosmology, while the fifth element was the divine essence conceived by Aristotle.

37. Šanda notes that trykdystiton is explained in the margin with tlty mtyn² and gives the Greek τριχοδιαστητον. The argument is based upon Philoponos' concept of space and place as the bearer of the form of matter with some differentiation between them. We need to be able to distinguish in the Alexandria Scientist the extension by which we conceive of empty space and the extension by which we conceive of body in place. Space is then given a dimension of depth which is related to time, whereby Philoponos can think together intangible and tangible realities.

38. The argument of the proper use of "in" and "of" for the universals and particulars of the Porphyrian Tree is grounded in the relation of form and matter in the cosmology of Philoponos. The Syriac is very pointed in the use of the prepositions and more vivid than English usage readily allows.

39. Cf. P. Gregorios, et al., ed., *Does Chalcedon Divide or Unite?* World Council of Churches, Geneva, 1981; B. L. Ramm, *An Evangelical Christology*, Thomas Nelson, New York, 1985, pp. 33-85; K. Barth, *Church Dogmatics,* vol. I, Part One, T. & T. Clark, Edinburgh, 1975, pp. 348-447.

40. W. Böhm, op. cit., pp. 61-62. Cf. Neidhardt, W. I., "The Creative Dialogue Between Human Intelligibility and Reality--Relational Aspects of Natural Science and Theology," The Asbury Theological Journal, Volume 41, Number 2, Fall, 1986, pp. 59-83, for the kind of effort we might make in this direction.

41. Ibid., pp. 262-64.

42. J. Kraemer, "A Lost Passage from Philoponus' Contra Aristotelem," JAOS LXXXV 85 (1965), pp. 318-27.

BIBLIOGRAPHY

Abel, A.
1968 "La Legende de Jean Philopon chez les Arabes," Cd'O X, pp. 251-80.

Abramowski, L., and Goodman, A. E.
1972 A Nestorian Collection. Cambridge: Cambridge University Press.

Allen, D.
1985 Philosophy for Understanding Theology. Atlanta: John Knox Press.

Altaner, B.
1960 Patrology. Tr. H. Graet. Freiburg: Herder.

Anderson, C.
1984 "The Integration of Platonism into Early Christian Theology." SP, vol. XV, pp. 399-413.

Armstrong, A. H., ed.
1967 The Cambridge History of the Later Greek and Early Medieval Philosophy. Cambridge: Cambridge UniversityPress.

Ayer, J. C.
1952 A Source Book for Ancient Church History. New York: Scribner's.

Bardy, G.
1924 "Jean Philopon." DTC VIII, 1, pp. 831-39.

Barth, K.
1975 Church Dogmatics, Vol. I, Part 1. Ed. G. W. Bromiley and T. F. Torrance. Edinburgh: T. & T. Clark.

Beckwith, J.
1970 Early Christian and Byzantine Art. London: Penguin Books.

Bell, H. I.
1927 "Alexandria." JEA XIII, pp. 171-84.

Blumenthal, H.
1982 "John Philoponus and Stephanus of Alexandria: Two Neoplatonic Christian Commentators on Aristotle?" In Neoplatonic and Christian Thought. Ed. D. J. O'Meara, International Society for Neoplatonic Studies, pp. 54-63.

Boas, G.
1961 Rationalism in Greek Philosophy. Baltimore: John Hopkins.

Böhm, W.
1967 Johannes Philoponos, Grammatikos von Alexandrien. München: Verlag Ferdinand Schöningh. [Contains a complete listing of all the manuscripts of Philoponos.]

Booth, E. G. T.
1983 Aristotelian Aporetic Ontology in Islamic and Christian Thinkers. Cambridge: Cambridge University Press.

149

1982 "John Philoponos: Christian and Aristotelian Conversion." In Studia Patristica, vol. I. New York, Pergamon Press, pp. 407-11.

Bromiley, G. W.
1979 "Christology." ISBE, vol. I. Grand Rapids, Michigan: Eerdmans, pp. 665-66.

1978 *Historical Theology: An Introduction.* Grand Rapids, Michigan: Eerdmans.

Browning, R.
1980 *The Byzantine Empire.* New York: Scribner's.

Chadwick, H.
1982a "Eucharist and Christology in the Nestorian Controversy." In *History and Thought of the Early Church.* London: Variorum, pp. 145-64.

1982b "Moschus and Sophronius." In *History and Thought of the Early Church.* London: Variorum, pp. 1-74.

1981 *Boethius.* Oxford: Clarendon Press.

1967 *The Early Church.* London: Penguin Books.

1954 *Alexandrian Christianity.* Philadelphia: Westminster Press.

Christensen, J.
1980 *Philoponos and Aristotle.* Ph.D. thesis, History of Science Department, Harvard University, Harvard, Massachusetts.

Clagett, M.
1955 *Greek Science in Antiquity.* New York: Collier.

Cohen, M. R., and Drabkin, I. E.
1948 *A Source Book in Greek Science.* New York: McGraw- Hill.

Coleman-Norton, P. R.
1966 *Roman State and Christian Church.* 3 volumes. London: SPCK.

Crombie, A. C.
1957 *Augustine to Galileo.* London: Heinemann.

1953 *Robert Grosseteste.* Oxford: Clarendon Press.

Cunliffe-Jones, H.
1978 *A History of Christian Doctrine.* Philadelphia: Fortress Press.

Danielou, J.
1961 *Message Evangelism et Culture Hellenistique.* Desclee et Cie.
Davidson, H. A.
1969 "John Philoponus as a Source of Medieval Islamic and Jewish Proofs of Creation." JAOS 89, pp. 357- 91.

Diehl, C.
1901 *Justinien et la Civilisation Byzantine au VI^eSiècle.* 2 volumes. New

York: Burt Franklin.

DeGroot, J.
1991   *Aristotle and Philoponus on Light.* New York and London: Garland Publishing, Inc.

Downey, G.
1958   "Justinian's View of Christianity and the Greek Classics." <u>ATR</u> 40, pp. 13-22.

Duhem, P.
1959   *Le Systeme du Monde.* Ten volumes. Paris: Hermann.

Ebied, R. Y.
1977   "Peter of Antioch and Damian of Alexandria: The End of a Friendship." *In A Tribute to Arthur Vööbus.* Ed. R. H. Fischer. Chicago: Lutheran School of Theology.

Ebied, R. Y., Van Roey, A., and Wickham, L. R.
1981   *Peter of Callinicum.* Leuven: Department Orientalistich.

Einstein, A.
1966   *The Evolution of Physics.* New York: Simon and Schuster. [Written to help his friend, Infeld, this is a fine attempt to put it into non-mathematical explication the significance of the development.]

1954   *Ideas and Opinions.* New York: Dell, Laurel Edition.

1950   *Essays in Physics.* New York: Philosophical Library.

1920   *Sidelights on Relativity.* New York: Dutton.

Evrard, E.
1965   "Jean Philopon, son Commentaire sur Nicomaque et ses rapports avec Ammonius." <u>REG</u> 78, pp. 596ff.

1953   "Les convictions religieuses de Jean Philopon et la date de son commentaire aux Meteorologiques." <u>BAB.L</u> XXXIX, pp. 299-357.

Farrington, B.
1969   *Science in Antiquity.* Oxford: Oxford University Press.

Forster, E. M.
1977   *Alexandria Still.* Princeton: Princeton University Press.

Forsyth, G. H.
1968   "The Monastery of St. Catherine at Mt. Sinai: The Church and Fortress of Justinian." <u>DOP</u> 22, pp. 3- 19.

Fouyas, M. G.
1976   *The Person of Jesus Christ in the Decisions of the Ecumenical Councils.* Ethiopia: Central Printing Press.

Frend, W. H. C.
1985   *Saints and Sinners in the Early Church.* Wilmington: Michael Glazier.

1984   *The Rise of Christianity*. Philadelphia: Fortress Press.

1972   *The Rise of the Monophysite Movement*. Cambridge: Cambridge University Press.

1966   *The Early Church*. Philadelphia: Lippincott.

Freeman, E. E.
1985   "The Rediscovery of Codex Syriacus." In Alumni/ae News, Princeton Theological Seminary, XXIV, 4 (Fall): 3-6.

Friedman, M.
1983   *Foundations of Space-Time Theories*. Princeton: Princeton University Press.

Furlani, G.
1923   "Unita e dualita de natura secondo Giovanni Filopono." Bess XXVII, pp. 45-65.

1921   "Il tratto di Giovanni Filopono sul rapporto tra le parti egli elementi ed il tutto e le parti." AIVS LXXXI, 2, pp. 83-105.

Furley, D.
1983   "Summaries of Philoponus' Corollaries on Place and Void." Conference on Philoponus, Institute of Classical Studies, London.

Gearakakoplos, D. J.
1984   *Byzantium*. Chicago: Chicago University Press.

Gerostergios, A.
1982   *Justinian the Great*. Belmont, Massachusetts: Institute forByzantine and Modern Greek Studies.

Gibson, M.
1981   *Boethius*. Oxford: Blackwell's.

Gonzalez, J. L.
1983   *A History of Christian Thought*. 3 volumes. Nashville: Abingdon Press.

Graffin, R., and Nau, F.
1973   "Letters of Severus." In *Patrologia Orientalis*, vol. 14 (nos. 67-71). Ed. and tr. E. W. Brooks, Belgique.

Gray, P. T. R.
1979   *The Defense of Chalcedon in the East*. Leiden: E. J. Brill.

Gregorios, P., Lazareth, W. H., and Nissiotis, N. A.
1981   *Does Chalcedon Divide or Unite?* Geneva: World Council of Churches.

Grillmeier, A., ed.
1954   *Das Konzil von Chalcedon*. Würzburg: Echter-Verlag.

Güdeman, A.

1916　"Ioannes Philoponus." In *Paulys Real Encyclopädie*. Ed. G. Wissowa and W. Kroll, Stuttgart, pp. 1764-1795. [Contains a complete bibliography of all the works of Philoponos.]

Guillanmont, A.
1969　"Justinien et l'Eglise de Perse." DOP 23, pp. 41-66.

Gunton, C. E.
1983　*Yesterday and Today*. Grand Rapids: Eerdmans.

Hardy, E. R.
1968　"The Egyptian Policy of Justinian." DOP 22, pp. 23-41.

Harnack, A.
1961　*The History of Dogma*. Dover and New York.

Henry, P.
1984　*Schools of Thought in the Christian Tradition*. Philadelphia: Fortress Press.

Hermann, Th.
1930　"Johannes Philoponus als Monophysit." ZNTW 29, pp. 209-64.

Herzog, J. J.
1856　"Johannes Philoponus." In Real-Encyklopadie, vol. 6, Stuttgart, pp. 760-63.

Hoffman, P.
1983　"Simplicius Against Philoponus on the Nature of the Heavens." Conference on Philoponus, Institute of Classical Studies, London.

Hussey, J. M., ed.
1966　*The Cambridge Medieval History*. Vol. 4. Cambridge: Cambridge University Press.

Hutter, I.
1971　*Early Christian and Byzantine Art*. New York: Universe Books.

John of Damascus
1958　*Writings*. Tr. F. H. Chase, Jr. New York: Fathers of the Church, Inc.

John Philoponos
1930　*Opuscula Monophysitica Ioannis Philoponi*. Ed. A. Šanda. Typographia Catholica PP. Soc. Jesu, Beryti Phoeniciorum (Beyrouth). Cf. Vaticanus Syriacus 144.

1535　*In primos quatuor Aristoteles*. Ed. B. Zanetti. Venedig. [Now at the Henry E. Huntington Library in Pasadena, California.]

Jaki, S. L.
1980　*Cosmos and Creator*. South Bend, Indiana: Regnery Gateway.

1978a　*The Origin of Science and the Science of Origin*. South Bend, Indiana: Regnery Gateway.

1978b *The Road of Science and the Ways to God.* Chicago: Chicago University Press.

1974 *Science and Creation.* New York: Science History Publications.

1966 *The Relevance of Physics.* Chicago: The University of Chicago Press.

Joannou, P.
1962 "Le premier essai chrevtien d'une philosophie systématique." <u>SP</u> V, p. 508.

Kelly, J. N. D.
1978 *Early Christian Doctrines.* New York: Harper & Row.

Kerrigan, A.
1952 *St. Cyril of Alexandria.* Roma: Pontificio Instituto Biblico.

Kraemer, J.
1965 "A Lost Passage from Philoponus' contra Aristotelem." <u>JAOS</u> LXXXV, pp. 318-27.

Lebon, J.
1909 *Le Monophysisme Severien.* Lovanii: Universitatis Catholicae Typographus.

Lovell, B.
1981 *Emerging Cosmology.* New York: Columbial University Press.

Mahdi, Muhsin.
1967 "Al-Farabi Against Philoponus." <u>JNES</u> 26, p. 352.

Malley, W. J.
1978 *Hellenism and Christianity.* Roma: Universita Gregoriana Editrice.

Mango, C.
1980 *Byzantium.* New York: Charles Scribner's Sons.

Martin, H.
1962 "Jean Philopon et la controverse tritheiste du VIe siècle." <u>SP</u>, vol. V, pp. 519-25.

Mascall, E. L.
1979 *The Relevance of Chalcedon Today.* Ed. C. C. Marcheselli, FS.

1966 *The Christian Universe.* New York: Morehouse-Barlow.

1965 *Christian Theology and Natural Science.* Archon Books, Longmans, Green & Co., Ltd. in United States of America.

McGuckin, J. A.
1984 "The 'Theopaschite Confession' (Text and Historical Context): A Study in the Cyrilline Re-interpretation of Chalcedon." <u>JEH</u> 35, 2 (April), pp. 239-55.

McKenna, J.E.

1986   "Christian Theology and Scientific Culture," <u>Studia Biblica et Theo-</u><u>logica</u>, Fuller Theological Seminary, pp. 133-143.

Meyendorff, J.
1975   *Christ in Eastern Christian Thought.* Athens: St. Vladimir's Press. (After my writing, *Imperial Unity and Christian Divisions: The Church 450-680 A.D.*, Crestwood, New York, 1989 as a very fine study.)

1968   "Justinian, the Empire, and the Church." <u>DOP</u> 22, pp. 45-60.

Meyerhof, M.
1931   "Joannes Grammatikos (Philoponos) von Alexandrien und die arabische Medizin." <u>MDIAA</u> II:2.

Moosa, M.
1986   *The Maronites in History.* New York: Syracuse University Press.

Nebelsick, H. P.
1985   *Circles of God: Theology and Science from the Greeks to Copernicus.* Edinburgh: Scottish Academic Press.

Neidhardt, W. J.
1986   "The Creative Dialogue Between Human Intelligibility and Reality--Relational Aspects of Natural Science." <u>The Asbury Theological Journal</u>, 41, 2, 1986, pp. 59-83.

Parsons, E. A.
1952   *The Alexandrian Library.* London: Cleaver-Hume.

Percival, H. R.
1971   *The Seven Ecumenical Councils.* Vol. XIV, Library of Nicene and Post-Nicene Fathers. Grand Rapids: Eerdmans.

Pines, S.
1972   "An Arabic Summary of a Lost Work of John Philoponus." In <u>Oriental Studies</u>, II (Tel Aviv University, Jerusalem: Central Press), pp. 320-52.

Reiner, H.
1954   "Der Metaphysik-Kommentar des Joannes Philoponos." <u>Hermes</u> LXXXII, pp. 396-410.

Saffrey, H. D.
1954   "Le chrevtien Jean Philopon et la survivance de l'Ecole d'Alexandrie en VIe siècle." <u>REG</u> LXVII, pp. 396-410.

Sambursky, S.
1975   *Physical Thought from the Presocratics to the Quantum Physicists.* Pica Press: New York. [This is the best survey that I know.]

1972   "Note on John Philoponus Rejection of the Infinite." In *Islamic Philosophy and the Classical Tradition.* Columbia, South Carolina: University of South Carolina Press, pp. 351-53.

1971   *The Concept of Time in Late Neoplatonism.* Jerusalem: The Israel Academy of Sciences and Humanities.

155

1967 "John Philoponos." In *The Encyclopedia of Philosophy*. Vol. 6. New York: Macmillan.

1962 *The Physical World of Late Antiquity*. New York: Basic Books.

1959 *The Physics of the Stoics*. New York: Mcmillan.

Samuel, V. C.
1977 *The Council of Chalcedon Re-examined*. Christian Literature Society, Indian Theological Library.

Šanda, A., ed.
1930 *Opuscula Monophysitica Ioannis Philoponi,* Beryt: Phoeniciorum, Typographia Catholica.

Sellers, R. V.
1961 *The Council of Chalcedon*. London: SPCK.

Sorabji, R.
1987 *Philoponus and the rejection of Aristotelian Science*. New York: Cornell University Press. [This is the major work published after the international conference held at King's College, London and after my writing.]

1983 *Time, Creation and the Continuum*. New York: Cornell University Press.

1982 "Infinity and the Creation." Inaugural Lecture. London: King's College.

1980 *Necessity, Cause, and Blame*. New York: Cornell University Press.

Strabo
1959 *The Geography*. Tr. H. L. Jones. London: Heinemann.

Stump, E.
1978 *Boethius' De topicis differentiis*. New York: Cornell University Press.

Taton, R.
1963 *History of Science*. Tr. A. J. Pomerans. New York: Basic Books.

Todd, R. B.
1980 "Some concepts in physical theory in John Philoponus' Aristotelian commentaries." Archiv für Begriffsgeschichte 24, pp. 151-70.

Torrance, I.R.
1988 *Christology After Chalcedon*. St. Mary's Plain, Norwich, Norfolk: The Canterbury Press. [Written after my dissertation, I believe Ian Torrance has made here clarification vitally needed for understanding the thought of Philoponos.]

Torrance, T. F.
1985a *Reality and Scientific Theology*. Edinburgh: Scottish Academy Press.

1985b *The Christian Frame of Mind*. Edinburgh: The Handsel Press.

1985c *Theological Dialogue Between Orthodox and Reformed Churches.*(Ed.) Edinburgh: Scottish Academy Press.

1984 *Transformation and Convergence in the Frame of Knowledge.* Grand Rapids: Eerdmans. [Just for its bibliography, this book is profoundly helpful.]

1983 "John Philoponos of Alexandria: Sixth Century Christian Physicist." Texts and Studies, vol. II, pp. 261-65.

1982 *Reality and Evangelical Theology.* Philadelphia: Westminster Press.

1981 *Divine and Contingent Order.* Oxford: Oxford University Press.

1980a *Christian Theology and Scientific Culture.* Belfast: Christian Journals Ltd.

1980b *The Ground and Grammar of Theology.* Charlottesville: University of Virginia Press.

1976 *Space, Time and Resurrection.* Grand Rapids: Eerdmans.

1975 *Theology in Reconciliation.* Grand Rapids: Eerdmans.

1969 *Space, Time and Incarnation.* Oxford: Oxford University Press.

1965 *Theology in Reconstruction.* Grand Rapids: Eerdmans.

Tixeront, J.
1948 *History of Dogma.* 3 volumes. Westminster, Maryland: Christian Classics.

Verbeke, G.
1966 *Jean Philopon.* Louvain: University of Louvain.

Wallace-Hadrill, D. S.
1982 *Christian Antioch.* Cambridge: Cambridge University Press.

1968 *The Greek Patristic View of Nature.* New York: Manchester University Press.

Walzer, R.
1962 "Greek into Arabic: Essays on Islamic Philosophy." In Oriental Studies, vol. I. Ed. S. M. Stern and R. Walzer. Oxford: Cassirer.

Westerink, L. G.
1964 "Deux Commentaires sur Nicomaque: Asclépius et Jean Philopon." Revue des Études Grecques 77, pp. 526-35.

Wieland, W.
1970 *Die Aristotelische Physik.* Göttingen: Vandenhoeck & Ruprecht.

1969 "Die Ewigkeit der Welt: Der Streit zwischen Philoponos und Simplicius." In *Die Gegenwart der Griechen im neueren Denken.* FS for H. G. Gadamer, Tubingen, pp. 291-316.

157

Wildberg, C.
1988   *John Philoponus' Criticism of Aristotle's Theory of Aether*. Berlin and New York: W. de Gruyter. [Written after my dissertation, the issue of the ether I believe ought to remain and open one within the contingency conceived by Philoponos and his three-dimensionality theory.]

Wilken, R. L.
1971   *Judaism and the Early Christian Mind*. Yale University Press (1968).

Wright, W.
1894   *A Short History of Syriac Literature*. London: Black.

Young, F. M.
1983   *From Nicea to Chalcedon*. Philadelphia: Fortress Press.